Moving to Spain with Child
for anyone thinking abo

M000010029

"The Bible for any parent aiming to live in Spain. Up-to-date, clear and full of vitally important information, Lisa's book is a 'must-have' for any parent considering moving to Spain or here now with their children". **Nick Snelling, Gandia (Author)**

"Essential reading for anyone considering moving to Spain with children, and in fact even without children, it is an excellent starting point…" **Kelly Lawlor, Vejer de la Frontera.**

"With so many factors to consider when moving to Spain, this book is indispensable reading for every family. From critical factors such as healthcare, tax and gaining an NIE, to personal decisions such as schooling, languages and location, every major issue facing relocating families is well covered." Caroline Angus Baker, New Zealand (Author).

"…if you are serious about making the move then you couldn't have a better guide in your hands than this book right here" **Maya Middlemiss, Denia, Alicante.**

"Lisa has produced an easy to read, yet invaluable guide for 'Moving to Spain with Children'." **Ali Meehan, Malaga (Founder of Costa Women - costawomen.com)**

"For many years, Lisa Sadleir has been offering credible, independent counsel to families considering relocating to Spain. This book offers a valuable overview, including honest and clear advice on important issues for a successful relocation…" **Andrew FORBES, Malaga. (Journalist, Consultant & Editor)**

All Rights Reserved

No part of this publication may be reproduced or transmitted by any means, electronic, mechanical, photocopy or otherwise, without the prior permission of the publisher. This is a work of non-fiction. Names, people, places and incidents are real and included by the author with consent, under editorial licence.

First published in Great Britain in 2014 by U P Publications Ltd
145-157 St. John Street, LONDON EC1V 4PW

Cover design copyright © U P Publications 2014
Using artwork with permissions under copyright © LOL MALONE 2014

Copyright © LISA SADLEIR 2014

Lisa Sadleir has asserted her moral rights

A CIP Catalogue record of this book is available from the British Library

Paper Back Edition
ISBN 978-1908135605

FIRST PAPERBACK EDITION

9 1 2 8 7 3 6 4 5 0

Published by U P Publications –
Printed in England by The Lightning Source Group

www.uppbooks.com
http://familylifeinspain.com

Moving to Spain with Children

Essential reading for
anyone thinking about moving to Spain

By Lisa Sadleir
Mijas, Spain 2014

2014
U P Publications Ltd

Dedication

This book is dedicated to my family.
Thank you for your never-ending belief and support.
Without you all, this wonderful journey
would not have been possible.

Here's to the next chapter…

Contents

Education 42

Introduction

Moving to Spain with Children
Essential Reading for Parents

Spain is a wonderful place to live. It is the place I have chosen to bring up my children. Having lived here for over 23 years now, I cannot envisage living anywhere else (although I will never say never!).

Living in Spain allows us, as a family, to appreciate that: we have more time with our children; we spend more time outdoors in the fresh open air; family comes first; material possessions are not important; people are generally very friendly and open; we are living an invaluable experience.

Every year, many people consider moving to Spain. Every year people make the move and sometimes it doesn't work out and they return home (you know, the stories often published in the tabloids and UK sensationalist TV programs). From experience, I am inclined to say that many failed relocations are due to inadequate research and incorrect advice (Health issues aside!).

Spain used to be a popular destination for young people looking for a new start and retirees hoping their pension would go further in warmer climes. Nowadays, with the change in the economic climate, more and more families who are financially independent are making the move. The majority of the people I agree to assist are looking for a better quality of life for their family.

The most common scenarios are that the parents have an online business and so are location independent, or, one of the parents works overseas in a job that means they are away for weeks or months at a time. These families are looking for a safe and enjoyable environment in which to live. There has also been a recent increase in the number of highly skilled professionals being recruited or relocated to Spain by larger companies who are setting up headquarters here, as a result of new business incentives.

So, if you are moving to Spain, without a secure income and looking for work, please rethink and contact me if you are uncertain.

If you are planning to move to Spain in search of a better family life, please read on...

Welcome to Moving to Spain with Children

The aim of the book is to

- Give you food for thought
- Provide factual info & sources of information
- Share real life experiences

Warning: If you are looking to be sold the dream, put this book down now and buy one of the many other books on the market.

This book is not here to sell you a dream.

This book will show you the reality.

This book will show you what life in Spain is really like.

This book will tell you what you need to think about before deciding to make the move.

This book will give you a much better start to your life in Spain.

This book will become your invaluable source of thinking material and insight, in preparation for your move and during your first months in Spain.

So, Who Am I?

My name is Lisa Sadleir, aka "mum" from Family Life in Spain and founder CCB Spain.

Having answered questions from many families thinking about moving to Spain, over the past years, and at the request of many mums, I decided it was time to put this book together.

I am British and currently living in the white-washed Andalusian village of Mijas, Malaga in southern Spain, with my British husband, two beautiful, bilingual children and a doting German Shepherd.

I have travelled and lived in different parts of mainland Spain and the Spanish islands since 1991.

I write about moving to and living in Spain on my websites:

www.familylifeinspain.com

www.ccbspain.com

www.movetomalaga.com

www.movetomijas.com

I regularly contribute to various expat magazines and websites.

My plan is for this book to answer a lot of your questions. In fact, I believe this book will answer questions you may not have even thought about. In the long run, this book will save you time, money and headaches and, without doubt, it will pay for itself many times over.

This book highlights the most important practical issues to be considered when moving to Spain with children.

It is not a psychological guide book, I believe that most parents understand their children well enough to know if they need to seek professional psychological guidance.

I believe this book will make the whole process of moving to Spain with children a lot more understandable and enjoyable. The majority of the information provided applies to all areas of Spain. Extra insight is given to the Malaga province where I have chosen to live with my own family.

Timing

"There is no one correct answer to 'When is the right age to move abroad with children?' However, this is a question you must ask yourself about your own personal situation."

The Importance of Timing

I'm sure most of you will have heard of the Real Estate 3 tips for a successful property purchase:

1. Location
2. Location
3. Location

On a similar note, my 3 tips for successfully moving abroad with children are:

1. Timing
2. Timing
3. Timing

Before, looking at these 3 tips in more detail, let's look at the concept of "time" and "timing".

Time is extremely important in our lives; it helps us structure our daily lives and activities, so that we can live more organised, productive and enjoyable lives.

While there are always drawbacks to being too conscious of time (such as the feeling of being "ruled by the clock"), it is essential that we have this marker to use while we work, play, grow older and make important life changing decisions.

This becomes even more crucial when we become parents and

have our children to care for and manage.

"Time only seems to matter when it's running out" – **Peter Strup**

Timing is a key factor to the success of many events in our lives. Knowing when to act is critical in anything we do. If we are aware of the importance of timing, we are more likely to be successful. However, if we ignore the importance of timing, achieving success becomes more of an uphill struggle.

It can be argued that timing is the state of affairs that determine whether we will be able to reach our goals or not. It can be the conditions we create or the hand that life has dealt to us at any given point. However, when planning on moving abroad with children, the hand of fate often plays a minor role.

Dictionary definitions: tim•ing (ˈtaɪ mɪŋ) (noun) – *the selecting of the best time for doing or saying something in order to achieve the desired effect. – the process or art of regulating actions or remarks in relation to others to produce the best effect, as in music, the theatre, sport.*

My experience is based on my dealings with families moving to Spain with children, however the general concepts can be applied to any country. There are three elements that I deem it is essential to consider when planning the timing of your move abroad:

1.   Timing: as in the right time in your child's life
2.   Timing: as in the time of year
3.   Timing: in relation to your own life

"The bad news is time flies. The good news is you're the pilot" -
Michael Althsuler

1. It's All About The Children

We are adults. We are responsible for our decisions and our actions. As parents, we are also responsible for the decisions we make for our children. This may seem obvious, but a recent survey I have conducted, about moving to Spain with children (by people who have already done it), brought some shocking truths to light.

There is no one correct answer to *"When is the right age to move abroad with children?"* However, this is a question you must ask yourself about your own personal situation.

Generally, younger children are more adaptable and open to change and therefore easier to move. If you are moving to a country that does not speak your native tongue, the younger the age of the child, the earlier they will adapt to the new language if they are immersed in it.

Older children may be more resistant to the idea of moving to another country due to leaving friends and of course the more complicated issues in terms of education. On the other hand, they understand a great deal more about different cultures, retain far more, and can therefore gain much more from the experience.

There are many online articles and guides about how to prepare your children for their move abroad, take time to read them and learn from other peoples experiences. Irrespective of age, the more time you spend planning your move and involving your children in your plans, the more likely you are to achieve success.

"We worry about what a child will become tomorrow, yet we forget that he is someone today." – **Stacia Tauscher**

2. What Time Of Year?

Provided you have a choice about when you move, (i.e. it is not subject to work demands, although that does not always have to dictate the timing of your child's move), the only way you can decide is by researching your chosen destination.

I am often surprised at the number of families who tell me that they are planning to move to Spain "just before Christmas" or "over the Christmas period". I cannot think of a worse time. Needless to say, their plans change following their first conversation with me.

Why do I consider this to be a bad choice?

In a nutshell; the weather, school timetables and Christmas celebrations!

Tip 1: Research the weather patterns of your chosen destination. Here in Southern Spain, the majority of people choose to move here for the sunnier climate and the wonderful outdoor lifestyle (amongst other factors of course!).

However, the weather is generally the most unreliable between the months of December and March.

As a result, you and your children will not be starting off in the best climatic conditions. Your promises of sunny days on the beach and outdoor lifestyle may well be questioned!

Tip 2: Research local and traditional celebrations in your new destination. Christmas and New Year is traditionally a time to be spent with friends and family. It is the most celebrated time of year in some countries but not in all.

Imagine, your first Christmas in your new destination where you do not know anybody, you may not even be able to buy a Christmas tree and all the gifts sent by post have not yet arrived.

Not an ideal situation for our loved ones, is it?

Tip 3: Research school term times and enrolment procedures. In Spain, school applications are generally submitted in March, places are confirmed by June and term starts in September.

So, why move over in December? Even in our home country, starting a child in a new school in the middle of the school year can be challenging.

Imagine starting them in a new school in a new country in the same circumstances.

Don't we at least want to try and make it easier for them?

In many countries, schools offer summer camps in the months of July and August, this is a great opportunity for your child to meet some of their new classmates-to-be, in a more relaxed and fun environment.

Why not check this out before finalising the planned time of your move?

"Time you enjoyed wasting is not wasted time." **T S Elliot**

3. Is this the right time for you?

People move abroad for many reasons. People also move back to their home county for many reasons. Unfortunately, not always the right reasons.

How do you know if this is the right time in your life to make the move? Ask yourself: What is my main reason for wanting to move abroad?

Work Commitments? Many people move abroad for work commitments. If this is your case, are you sure that taking the children with you is the best choice? Have you considered commuting? Many families live very happy lives like this.

Check out the alternatives and ensure that your new destination is suitable for your children. Does it offer the opportunities you want for them?

Looking for new job opportunities for yourself? This is a difficult one, especially in the current economic climate. I am currently advising people not to move to Spain unless they are financially independent or they have secured a guaranteed work contract.

In search of a better lifestyle? This is thankfully the main reason people tell me. It is the reason I most love to hear. It is the reason I live where I live. It is the reason I love my work.

"Whatever you want to do, do it now! There are only so many tomorrows." **Pope Paul VI**

So there you have it. I hope you do not feel I have preached. My aim is merely to give you food for thought, questions to ask yourself and to drive home the importance of research, planning and timing.

We are always told that we learn by making mistakes. However, many mistakes can be avoided by learning from others who made the move and who are ready to help you. You only have to ask…

Timing: Our Story

Throughout the rest of the book, we will be sharing "Our Story" with you. These are incidents and experiences taken from our family blog www.familylifeinspain.com.

The aim of sharing our stories with you is to show you the rough with the smooth. We will prepare you for the type of obstacles you may have to overcome when living in Spain. Despite being a stickler for learning the intricacies of the Spanish bureaucratic system, I often come up against what appears to be a brick wall. But, where there's a will, there's a way. If I present you with a possible problem, I will also provide you with a solution and a reason to smile.

In this first "Our Story", it is actually "Blake's Story" ….

As you have just read, in the previous "Timing" chapter, all children are individual. One rule does not suit all. The successful adaptation of your child to Spanish life and, in particular, Spanish education does not necessarily depend on the age of your child.

I am often asked by parents if their child is too old to try Spanish education. As I have already said, that is something that they have to decide, taking into consideration all the information I give them.

Blake's Story

About three years ago, Blake's family, who were in the process of moving to Mijas Pueblo, requested my help regarding Blake's education. At that time, he was 13 years old. They were keen to fully integrate into village life and were considering the state secondary school in the village.

Despite nobody speaking much Spanish, Blake included, the desire to integrate and the open willingness to learn made the state education a viable option. Blake's parents made it very clear to Blake that, should he be accepted at the school, he would very likely repeat his first year due to his lack of language ability. Would he mind this? Did he understand the implications, particularly with friendships and classmates?

We visited the school and Blake was accepted. He did repeat a year, as we forewarned him. But how did he get on? Did they make the right decision?

I asked Blake to tell it in his own words. What is printed here is exactly as he sent it to me. Nothing has been altered. This is simply to demonstrate what I have already said. All children are individual. You know your children. They are adaptable. Only you can decide what you feel is best for them. It is your decision.

Over to Blake

"Well, first of all when we landed here I didn't have a clue of what I was expecting, I went straight to my new house and decided that I needed to go and make some friends, so that's what I did.

I got on my bike and cycled into the village and kept on cycling around until I found someone that looked about my age, this was going to be a struggle because I could hardly say "hola", so I went up to this kid and I said "hola" and then I thought, I'm stuffed I don't know anything else to say!

This is when I decided to say bye even that was difficult, because I didn't know how to say bye in Spanish! Well that was on Monday on Wednesday I started school, Spanish school, that is the way forward! Personally the worst thing you can do is go to an English school. 3 reasons why:

1) It's very, very expensive.

2) You will never learn Spanish.

3) You will never feel comfortable living in Spain.

I shall explain that last comment, if you go to a spanish school, you get in with the Spanish culture, you have Spanish friends you get invited to lots of places and it's a fantastic lifestyle.

Well going back to my first day at school, this was quite a scary thing to do but because I had gone into the village and showed my face to the people, people recognised me straight away and started to introduce me to everyone I started to feel more confident and I made new friends after that school was the last of my worries, school is a really, really nice environment to be in here in Spain.

The teachers are lovely, they treat you as if you're their friend not as if you're a student which is a nice change.

I've been living here now 3 years and I am fluent in Spanish, I took it to heart and decided that I needed to learn Spanish to get on here, I've had such a laugh learning Spanish, people really appreciate you trying.

I'm not going to lie it wasn't easy but I got there in the end, I hit a point that I thought, "I'm not going to be able to do this it's too hard" but when you get to that point!

Don't give up because it will come all in its time you just need to give it some patience and you will get it! Another tip that I can give you and this was the best tip that anyone ever gave me was DO NOT mix with the English kids otherwise you will NEVER learn Spanish and trust me, it's true!"

NOTE: Blake's feelings about attending a Spanish state school rather than an International school are very strong. This does not mean that it would be the same for your child. We will look at the education options in a later chapter and will provide you with factors to consider when making your own decision.

Location

"... whether you are looking to invest money in a property or a simply looking for a rental property, choosing the correct location is fundamental to, not only the success of your move, but also your future happiness in your new home."

Location, Location, Location!

I'm sure many of you have watched the property programmes on the TV. You know, the ones that stress the importance of finding the correct location when considering buying a new house. (As also referred to in the previous chapter!)

In my opinion, and speaking from experience, whether you are looking to invest money in a property or a simply looking for a rental property, choosing the correct location is fundamental to, not only the success of your move, but also your future happiness in your new home.

This is also why I encourage you to rent before buying when first starting a new life in Spain. Yes, I agree that rent can be dead money. However, until you are certain you have the correct location for you, the dead rental paid will probably be a lot less that the expense incurred by the purchase of the wrong property.

If, however, you know the area you want to move to and have spent a lot of time there, then purchasing a property may be your best option. Think about using an independent property finder to help you choose the best location and best property for you.

From experience, when you approach an estate agent selling a particular property in a particular area, you may not always get the whole picture. A good, independent property finder or relocation advisor will be impartial to commissions. They will work for you and help you secure the most suitable location for your home in Spain.

Basic Factors To Consider

Basic factors to take into consideration when deciding on your location are accessibility and available infrastructure: What is the nearest airport? How frequent are the flights to your preferred destinations? It goes without saying that, once you have moved over, there will be an influx of visitors. Not only that, if you need to return back to your home country at short notice, it is comforting to know how easy it is.

Without wanting to sound morbid, we need to consider the age and health of our family and friends. Moving away is exciting, but bad news from back home can have a drastic impact on this excitement and the happiness of your family. Knowing you can easily pop back, if necessary, at a short notice, gives many people peace of mind.

If one of the parents travels frequently for work, proximity to the airport is very important. As a guideline, I would suggest not more than an hour's drive or a short train ride away. Commuting can eat into your day and eventually wear you down. You are not moving here for that.

The weather and climatic variations: Although Spain has a wonderful climate, there are regional variations, particularly in the winter months. Do not make the mistake of believing that it is always sunny in Spain. Believe it or not, despite the South of the country generally having the warmest climate and the best all year round average temperatures, the wettest place in Spain is actually in Grazalema, a village located in the north-eastern part of the province of Cádiz, in southern Spain.

In some parts of Spain, the winter months can be long and harsh and the summers dry and hot, particularly in more rural, mountainous locations. Many properties are not built to cater for these temperature changes.

Keep this in mind when considering both places to live and properties.

It is also worthwhile remembering that two weeks in Spain, in the heat and the sunshine, can be very enjoyable and relaxing when on holiday. However, is this what you are looking for on a daily basis? Research. Be informed. Be prepared.

The type of environment: Are you looking for a big, bustling city that offers an abundance of cultural activities? Are you dreaming of a beautiful, quaint, sleepy Spanish village? Whatever your ideal location, it is important to ask yourself a few questions:

- How important is it that there are people of your own nationality in the area?

- If you are looking at a typically Spanish village, might language be an issue?

- If you live in a more touristy area, what will it be like in the height of summer and also in the winter?

- Are there cinemas, activity centres, museums nearby to keep you and the children entertained?

- What activities are available when the weather is bad?

Education and Schools: This goes without saying! Whether you intend to send your children to a Spanish State school or a private, International school make sure you research the education options before looking for a property. I will talk more about education and the school system in a later chapter.

Property Prices: Consider what you can afford. Property prices vary greatly, not only in each area of Spain but also within neighbouring villages and towns. Have a look online to see what average prices are in the areas you are considering.

I encourage people to set a comfortable budget and then to see what they are able to achieve within that budget[1]. You may be amazed by the difference in prices within short geographical areas. Again, this is where the knowledge of a local property finder or relation adviser can be invaluable.[2]

The basic factors to consider when deciding what type of property to choose are:

Type of property: i.e. Apartment / townhouse / villa: Remember that spending a couple of weeks on holiday in an apartment is not like daily living. Think about how much space you are used to. Do remember, that in most parts of Spain, a lot of time is spent outdoors. Research the different options available in the areas you are considering.

Minimum number of bedrooms and minimum number of bathrooms: Do you want the children each to have their own room? Do you want to have spare rooms for guests to stay? In all honesty, think of yourselves first. Do not lose the house that you like because it does not have a guest room. Children can share when family and friends come to visit or holiday rentals are usually easy to find.

Build size and Plot size: How much space do you really need? How much are you going to have to pay in utility bills and

---

[1] NOTE: A long term rental contract in Spain is generally 11 months, although some owners will agree to a 6 month contract. Any shorter terms will be considered as short term or holiday rentals and will usually be charged on a weekly rate. Ensure you clarify contract lengths when enquiring about rental prices.

[2] If you are renting, I advise you to set a monthly budget to cover both rent and education fees. In some areas, you will be able to afford private education and rent within your budget. I am often shocked at people planning to spend up to €2500 per month on a rental property yet are unwilling to pay for their children's education (when deemed necessary due to age and language ability). Private education is often a lot cheaper in Spain compared to the UK

maintenance costs? A large villa may look appealing but large properties often mean large utility bills. Also, a pretty country house with lots of land may seem like a dream, but who will be looking after all that land? Remember to think with your head and not only your heart!

Garden and Swimming Pool: Private or communal? Again, think of your own privacy requirements or the opportunity of meeting other children in communal facilities. Communal facility charges are usually included in the price of a rental property but garden and pool maintenance are an extra cost to private villa rentals.

Distance from amenities / school / airport / beach: Are you happy to drive every day or do you prefer to be within reach of public transport or maybe walking distance of amenities. If the children's school provide transport, find out the routes before deciding on a property. If you will be commuting back to the UK or abroad on a regular basis, consider the commute time.

Budget: This is the most important factor to consider. Calculate your budget and stick to it. Research what kind of property you can hope to rent in the area you are considering.

These are just some of the many factors you should think about when planning your move. I hope they give you plenty to think about. If you are considering moving to the Malaga area, one of the first things I will ask you to do is to complete an initial relocation questionnaire that will give you plenty of food for thought.

Language

"I honestly believe that being able to speak at least a small amount of Spanish really contributes to your enjoyment of Spanish life."

The Importance of learning Spanish before Moving to Spain

In my opinion, too many people move to Spain without learning to speak Spanish. I'm not saying you need to be fluent but I am suggesting that it should be a personal goal to at least make a really big effort. Being able to at least start a conversation with a Spaniard, in their own language, will truly enhance your chances of integration and open so many more exciting doors for you.

"It is essential. Not speaking Spanish in Spain is just not living in Spain." **Pierre Alban-Waters (Madrid)**

I honestly believe that being able to speak at least a small amount of Spanish really contributes to your enjoyment of Spanish life. Spanish people are generally very warm and welcoming and genuinely seem to appreciate any attempt a foreigner makes to speak their language.

I appreciate that some people find it easier to learn a language than others but I find it hard to understand those who do not even try.

Admittedly, in many places, particularly in the popular coastal areas, speaking Spanish is not an absolute must as these places are so cosmopolitan and multi-national that Spanish is sometimes the least heard language. In many parts of Spain, particularly in areas where there are large expat communities, English is widely spoken and you can live a great life without needing to know a word of Spanish, if that is what you are looking for. However, a basic knowledge of Spanish can really make a dramatic difference.

"I think you can hit the ground running if you have 1) very basic Spanish, 2) a commitment to continuing study and 3) the right attitude (i.e. getting out there and getting things done despite the communication barrier, and OWNING the communication barrier rather than blaming it on "the Spanish") **Robin Graham (Tarifa)**

In some, mainly coastal areas, residents of all nationalities have set up their own little communities, shops, bars, restaurants and even schools. In contrast, in more rural areas and in the many, lovely, pueblos blancos (whitewashed villages), the inability to speak some Spanish may become a real burden upon your daily life.

I am not suggesting that you go back to school and study for an official qualification. I am simply suggesting that maybe by signing up for an evening class, buying a self-study book or even browsing some of the many online resources, you will pick up a little bit of the language and you will be thankful you did.

"My accent is Russian and my grammar is bad but I have a good vocabulary. Find I am forgiven much for trying. I think it is very necessary if you want quality of life and many friends. Learning Spanish to a good level takes a great many more hours than ads would lead us to believe" **Fiona Pitt-Kethley (Cartagena)**

Think About Your Children!

A scenario we see almost every day, living in Spain, is young children taking the lead in bars, restaurants and other places.

Can you imagine living in a place where your children are more in control than you are? A place where you have to ask your children to help you with simple day to day tasks. Imagine being in a situation where your children can have conversations with others and you have no idea what they are talking about.

"Interestingly ...in this area, the men struggle much more than the women due to a greater fear of making a fool of themselves (according to several blokes I asked). It's not that they don't know any Spanish, just not willing to look like an idiot.... kind of like the stereotype of not asking for directions!" **Yolanda Solo (Huelva)**

Ok, that may seem a little bit extreme.

However, I encourage you to think about it. Too many people do not.

Yes, I agree, it is a great way to encourage independence and boost confidence in our children but that is not always what it is. It is often due to their parents' lack of language knowledge.

People become lazy.

They rely on their children's amazing language learning ability.

But is that right?

Is that what you envisage for your family's future?

"Language is fundamental for understanding a country and for enjoying every aspect of a country and its people.

Whilst an expat is very rarely bilingual (as I understand it to be bilingual you have to be able to speak both languages as a native would of those countries) so fat chance most of us have even if you have been here years most of us have accents and make mistakes but of course you can you can get to a good level by going to classes, mixing, working in and practising Spanish daily. Spanish friends are a must." **Paddy Waller (Valencia)**

Not Everyone In Spain Speaks Spanish (Castilian)

The most common language in Spain is Spanish, also known as Castilian. However there are actually four more recognised, co-official languages in Spain: Catalan and its variant, Valencian, Gallego / Galician, Euskara / Basque and Arense / Occitan.

The reason for bringing this to your intention is to highlight the impact this may have, not only on your own daily life in Spain, but also on your children's education.

Hundreds of reports and research papers have been published advocating the support for preserving minority languages and dialects. People speak of the importance of preserving the history and romance of these beautiful languages.

History and romance aside, let's think of our children again ...

Speaking another language can improve your chances of love, earn you more money, make travel more fun and make you cleverer and healthier ... or so they say! Scientific studies have proven that speaking more than one language has many benefits in terms of travel, love, intelligence and money.

Four of the many declared key benefits of learning languages are:

- **Money** People who have more than one language earn more.
- **Love** Bilingual people are more attractive.
- **Travel** Is easier and more fun.
- **Intelligence** Bilingual people are smarter and healthier.

There are numerous interesting facts such as 270 British dating agencies have agreed that people who speak a foreign language are more attractive to the opposite sex and multilingual employees can expect a salary uplift of up to 20% in certain jobs.

However, on a more serious note, you must consider how having to learn not one but two new languages may affect your child. Do you think they will be able to cope? Will you be able to cope?

So What Can You Do to Start Learning Spanish?

I have previously used these self-study books available from Amazon and would happily recommend them:

BBC Sueños World Spanish 1 Course Book
BBC Sueños World Spanish 1 Activity Book
BBC Sueños World Spanish 1 Language Pack & CDs

I'm a true believer "sub conscious learning", playing lessons in the background, in the kitchen, whilst you're driving and in any other suitable situation. It is incredible what your brain picks up without you even realising it. The BBC material involves listening, reading and writing. The listening material is pretty authentic and will give you a good idea about pronunciation.

Watch Spanish cartoons with your children. Check out children's learning materials and participate in the classes with your children. Make it a fun family activity rather than a chore. The speed at which your children pick up the vocabulary and the accent will amaze you.

A couple of the many online resources I like are:

http://www.fun-learning-spanish.com/
http://www.learnspanish4life.co.uk/

A relatively newer learning method is online learning via Skype. I think this is a great method that will suit many people. No more excuses!

Skype language classes with a native teacher are available via Speak Up Spanish (http://www.intensivespanishonline.com/) and Alberto Professor (http://albertoprofesor.com/) amongst others.

With Skype language classes, students are encouraged to trust the flexible methods adopted to develop their communicative competences in the Spanish language. Customised learning systems support you during your study. With video conferences and other interesting tools, you will learn the most difficult issues of the language. Forget books and software, these courses welcome you into a virtual classroom.

Good reasons to choose online Skype language classes:

• Interesting courses that adapt to your needs.

• Courses are flexible, you can study from anywhere. You only need a computer and broadband internet service.

• You will learn Spanish with a personal teacher who will guide and motivate you.

• Teachers are native and have a university degree in Philology.

• All material is designed and evaluated by the academy manager.

• Interesting learning material and tools that will enhance your learning.

• Free sessions with your teacher and peers in order to deal with difficult topics of the language.

• Affordability and flexible payment options

If you are an app lover, then you need to have a look at http://www.busuu.com/mobile/kids – *busuu* is an innovative online community for learning languages. Like me, they suffered from using the traditional way to learn a new language which they found expensive, difficult and boring. As a result, they decided to create a new concept of language learning by offering you the following advantages:

• Learn from native speakers: Learn directly from native speakers of the *busuu* community via their integrated video-chat application. By doing so you can practice your language skills in a live conversation.

• Learn with their material: They have prepared over 150 learning units covering diverse topic areas and grammar units covering the most important grammar points! The content is image and sound-based.

• Learn for free: *busuu* can be used completely for free! However, you have the option to pay a minimal monthly fee to become a

Premium Member. With that Premium Membership you gain access to additional functionalities and more material.

busuu even offer a Business Spanish course for anyone needing to use Spanish in their professional lives.

Another great online resource for children is www.speekee.com

Speekee is an educational game where children from around the globe learn Spanish together in a safe online environment. A Spanish 'challenge' guides children through the whole language learning process from zero Spanish to a level of fluency. The challenge features fun games, videos with real Spanish children in real Spanish locations, safe live chat with 'friends', and virtual rewards. Instructions are in English and all gameplay is in Spanish. Established in 2006, *Speeke*e has grown to become one of the most comprehensive Spanish learning resources for children, anywhere on the Internet. Try it for free! www.speekee.com

If you prefer a full immersion option, then consider *Pueblo Español*.

Pueblo Español is an immersion course especially designed to expose the students to as much speaking Spanish as possible in a week's time! The activities are oriented and organised for a complete immersion in the Spanish language.

What does it involve?

- 8 day stay in a stunning location
- 1-to-1 ratio of native Spanish-speakers per student
- Different Spanish language accents
- More than 100 hours of learning experience while speaking Spanish
- Local excursions and time to explore the historical heritage village
- A stimulating and entertaining atmosphere
- Optional: SPECIAL PACK 8-day *PUEBLO ESPAÑOL*

plus 4-day SPANISH CLASSES
- Breakfast, lunch and dinner
- Transport to and from the venue (from Madrid, Spain)
- A schedule designed and organised so students gain confidence in their comprehension and communication skills

RESULTS

A noticeable improvement in listening and communication skills, as well improving self-confidence when speaking. For more information visit: http://www.diverbo.com/en/adult/spanish/spanish-intensive

So, what are you waiting for? It´s never too soon to start learning Spanish.

Oh! But be warned ...a simple "Hola ¿Qué tal?" to a local may result in a full blown conversation, if maybe one sided, about their life history... Welcome to my Spain!

Language: Our Story Part One

All you need to get started are a few words, some confidence and a smile …

Some teachers may disagree with me, however I believe that if you want to learn to converse in Spanish then you will be able to. Push all previous language learning failures aside, start afresh and buckle in.

My belief in your language learning ability stems from my own personal experience. I didn't have it easy when I first moved abroad. I was actually a student in a French business school. My French language teacher, an embarrassment to her profession, sucked the little confidence I had in her lessons. She openly mocked my accent when I read out loud. She reduced me to a nervous wreck in front of my follow students and any other French speaking person.

Despite having achieved an "A" at A level, (yes it was a few years ago!), I was made to feel useless. I clammed up and took almost eighteen months to learn to ignore her belittling treatment. Luckily, I befriended a lovely French lady at my work experience in Paris and my confidence was slowly rebuilt.

When I first moved to Spain, as a holiday guide in Gran Canaria, I was determined to learn the language and not let anybody belittle me like that again.

My first memory is of walking into a tabac to buy stamps for postcards to send back home and saying to the little man behind the counter "¿Cómo se dice esto en español?" whilst pointing at the stamp.

That day I learnt the word "sello" and made a friend to converse with. I didn't understand hardly anything else that he blurted out to me but it gave me confidence and determination. I could do this. It remains a very vivid memory.

Over the years, during my travels, I have studied for TEFL and taught English to Spanish students of all ages. I have designed a series of Spanish language classes for foreigners living in Spain.

I can now happily say that I am confident conversing in Spanish. I am in no way bilingual nor are my conversations grammatically correct. I am however, able to stand my own in most situations, argue my case and have no fear in language failure.

From all my experiences, I would like you to just take away one thing … CONFIDENCE. Have confidence in your own ability. Don't be scared to open your mouth and make mistakes. Muttering a badly constructed Spanish sentence in the totally wrong tense is much more likely to make you friends than you can imagine. Think of me and give it a try.

Language: Our Story Part Two

When deciding which part of Spain and even the UK to move to, our shortlist boiled down to the Girona region in Catalunya, the Angelsey region of North Wales and the Malaga region in Andalucía.

Weather aside, we had one other main influencing fact that left Malaga as our first choice: the language.

In Andalucía the children are taught in Castilian, in Girona they would learn both Castilian and Catalan, in Wales they would have to learn Welsh.

I am ducking for cover as I write this next comment.

Despite all the other factors that attracted us to the other regions, we did not want to subject our children to learning, what we considered to be, unnecessary languages.

Languages that we deemed solely necessary for them to be educated in a specific part of a country.

I am in no way saying that this is the correct decision for everyone, but having worked in Catalunya and being proficient in both French and Spanish, I did not see the need for introducing Catalan into our lives.

…As for trying to learn Welsh …

As I say, this is a very personal decision and one only you, as a parent, can make for your children. The benefits in the long run are incredible but the short run obstacles may hinder what may be a successful new start. You need to decide what is best for you.

Education

"Carefully research the schools in the area you plan to make your new home, before you plan your move to Spain."

What are Your School Options and How Do You choose?

Choosing the best kind of education in Spain for your children is one of the most important decisions you will make.

We all do what we believe is best for our children, yet how do we make the best choice regarding the right schools and types of education in Spain?

Rules and regulations differ. In Spain, there are no league tables to advise us which are the best performing schools, although there are many regulatory bodies that can be consulted to conduct basic checks.

Probably the biggest worry when moving abroad to Spain, is that you cannot always rely on the strong network of family and friends for practical experience, advice and guidance.

Whichever part of Spain or the islands you are moving to, or living in, you need to consider your own basic requirements, such as:

• Is your child better suited to a small or large school?

• Do you prefer them to change schools as they progress or stay in the same (For example the jump to senior school or the potential change at sixth form level)

• How far do you want your children to travel to school?

• What transport options exist / are provided by the school?

• What timetable best suits your own commitments?

• Do you prefer your children to have meals in school or will they come home to eat?

• Are the availability of extra-curricular activities important to you?

• Which language do you prefer your children to be educated in?

• Do you prefer a particular curriculum / teaching syllabus?

Factors to Consider When Deciding the Best For Your Child

One of the first decisions is whether to enrol your children in a Spanish state school or a private international school.

The availability of state schools and international schools in Spain varies by region. Hence, it is advisable to carefully research the schools in the area you plan to make your new home, before you plan your move to Spain.

When choosing a school in Spain for your children, the following factors should be considered:

The age of your child: From experience, this is only my personal opinion and to be taken or left as you choose, I would highly recommend enrolling any child aged 6 years or below in a Spanish state or Spanish speaking private school, whether it be a nursery or primary school. At this age they are sponges and you may be amazed at how quickly they integrate and pick up the language. I clearly remember our son´s first word after only a few days ... "mío" (mine)!

Your knowledge of the Spanish language: I am lucky to have a pretty high level of Spanish and my husband has a good conversational level. However, we often have to use Google in order to complete our 7-year-old's homework assignments. I truly believe that many expat children struggle in school due to the lack of available support at home, as a result of a lack of language ability.

My advice would be that once you are unable to help your children with their Spanish homework then you should consider either moving them to a private/international school or, as a more economical alternative, source a home tutor.

Financial commitments: Private schools are not cheap. State education is a much cheaper option. This school year we have seen quite a sharp increase in foreign students joining our children's state school.

Unfortunately, these are not children that have just relocated, these are older children that were previously in private international schools who, due to the downturn in their parents' economic position, have been forced to end their private education. Needless to say, they do not find it easy. This is not to say that any child older that 6 or 7 will not adapt. Children are amazing and they never cease to amaze us.

Your desired level of integration in Spanish life: This may seem like a strange consideration, however, we have met many people that have no interest whatsoever in integrating with the local Spaniards. Their children have attended private schools and have picked up the language randomly, as children do, by chatting with other Spanish children.

As a result, their children have integrated in a minor way in their town / village, yet, the parents continue to mix in their own circles.

I am in no way stating that if your children do not attend a Spanish state school that you will not integrate.

Nor am I saying that by putting your children in the local school will you be accepted as part of the local community.

In our village, everyone seems to know our children and I have worked hard at always being involved in meetings, school trips and activities in order to be accepted by the local mums.

Now, after almost 3 years, we seem to be considered as part of the community. As a parent, you need to decide what you want and what you think is best for your child and your family.

School Timetables: In Andalucía, the state school timetable for lessons is 9am until 2pm. In most schools, there is a canteen option (at extra cost) and extra-curricular activities (at extra cost) and an early morning drop-off option (at extra cost). In other parts of Spain the schools close for a 2 hour lunch and continue lessons in the afternoon. Private/International schools tend to follow the traditional UK timetables of 9am until 4pm or 5pm.

Whichever type of school you choose, do consider the implications of the timetable and transportation options. It is very easy to soon get fed up of spending half your time as a school taxi.

These are only 5 of many considerations when selecting a school for your child but I believe they will help you to start deciding which path you wish to follow and will set you in the right direction.

The Different Types of Schools in Spain

The first and maybe easiest option of education in Spain that you can dismiss is home-schooling. Why? Basically because it is illegal in Spain to home school. However there are possibilities to do it if you can be considered a diplomat with a child. Take a look at this website (http://www.wikihow.com/Homeschool-Your-Children) if you are interested.

Next there is the option of choosing Spanish state school education. Spanish state education is good in the sense that it socialises the child really well and is fundamental in the language learning process.

However, it can be argued that state education is suffering a lot at the moment due to the savage cuts being put in place by the government both to staff numbers and to facilities including books. We will explain the state system in more detail later in this section.

(Note: On a personal note, we continue to be very happy with the level of education provided at our children's state school and are impressed with the variety of subjects and teaching methods used.)

The next option is known as the concertado system. This is kind of a halfway house between state and private education. Originally the concertado schools were mostly religious. However, that is no longer always the case. There is a cost involved in sending your child to a concertado school but generally the costs are less than that of private schools. Again, it must be stated that concertado schools are also currently suffering from government cuts as they are dependent on government money to subsidise the cost of their education.

Last but not least we can consider Private schools: the most popular being International schools in Spain and the fully private Spanish schools.

The fully private Spanish schools follow the curriculum of the Spanish state system. However the teacher pupil ratio tends to be lower and also they tend to have better facilities. The school fees charged by fully private Spanish schools are similar to those of International Schools. It should be noted that the majority of the fully private Spanish schools are religious in nature.

The International Schools in Spain follow the curriculum of a particular country or the International baccalaureate. In most parts of Spain it is possible to find British, American, German, French and Scandinavian schools. In general, Spanish families send their children to the British schools for education because they believe that knowing English from a European country is a better option for the children. However there are certain areas of Spain where the American schools have very good reputations and also the French schools and German schools can also be recommended.

In today's world the English language is now accepted as the language of business and commerce. Therefore it is quite typical for Spanish families to want to send their children to English-speaking schools. This means that in many parts of Spain there is high demand for English school education. This can result in waiting lists and it may be impossible to get a place at your preferred school.

Again, I would like to stress the importance of research. Ensure you check the availability in your chosen school before finalising any property arrangements.

Introducing the Spanish State School System

The Spanish Education System – (for ages 3 to 16)

I think that every village and town, of any size, will have a primary school. The schools may vary considerably in size and sophistication, but they are known to provide a caring and friendly environment for small children. Most will take children in the year that they turn three.

Some state schools in certain areas of Spain only teach in the dialect of the given region, as opposed to in Spanish. So, in Catalonia, Galicia, Valencia or the Basque country subjects are taught in respectively Catalan, Gallego, Valencian or Basque. This is not always the case but is something to investigate carefully, as it will mean that your child will be taught in the regional dialect before learning Spanish. That said, most children master both the local dialect and Castellano (Spanish) as part of their general schooling.

Exposing children to several languages, at an early age can be very beneficial

The initial State School system is split into:

Pre-school (Educación Infantil) for ages 3 to 6 years

Primary School (Colegio): First Cycle for ages 6 to 8 years, and Second Cycle for ages 8 to 10 years.

Pre-school in Spain (Educación Infantil)

Pre-school in Spain (Educación Infantil), is a non-compulsory option available for children aged 3 to 6 years.

Children enter pre-school in the autumn of the year in which they turn 3 years old, hence why pre-school classes are often referred to as the class of: 3 años, 4 años and 5 años.

Although not obligatory, pre-school is considered an integral part of a child´s education. Even though there are no rigid targets, the children are introduced to subject matters that they go on to study in more detail in Primary School, they learn to interact with others and learn to adapt to routines. This is also the age at which children subconsciously absorb new language.

Both our children have been educated at the Educación Infantil level in a Spanish state school. Our initial experiences with both of them were very different, however, as time passes by, we can see we made the right decision and would strongly encourage other parents, whenever possible, to send their young children to Educación Infantil in a state run school.

Tip 1: It may not be easy at the start but it should make the transition to compulsory education a lot easier and less stressful … particularly for your children.

Tip 2: Entry to a primary school depends upon the catchment area in which you live. So, make sure you find a satisfactory school for your children before buying a property - otherwise you may find that your children are not eligible to go to the school of your preferred choice.

Primary School (Colegio) (ages 6 to 12 years)

This is the point at which I strongly recommend you consider all options for your child. At age six, the obligatory educational phase begins.

The children study subjects such as Spanish language (Lengua), mathematics, nature and environment (conocimiento del medio), religion (based on your choice), English language, music and physical education.

There are tests (controles) every few months. Failure to pass these tests throughout the year may result in your child having to repeat the year.

As school hours are quite short in state school, any unfinished classroom work must be completed at home. If your child is a slow worker or has comprehension issues, you may find they have a lot of homework. Many expat parents can be heard complaining about the silly amounts of homework that their children bring home. Not all of them are aware that it is often because their child is not working hard in the classroom!

This brings me to another point … the language.

If your child appears to be struggling at school, you need to be able to speak to the teachers to understand why.

Not all teachers speak a decent level of English. So, you will be better off speaking Spanish or have somebody that can translate for you.

As in the UK, our children need our support at home with their education, you need to decide if you would be capable of supporting your child in Spanish. If not, what other alternatives do you have?

Not speaking fluent Spanish should not deter you from giving you children to benefit from Spanish state education, however you should consider taking on support from others. It is not unusual for schools to offer out of hours classes to help children with their homework. In many places there are private after school groups that offer the same. Another great way is to pay a local teenager or even qualified tutor to come to your home to help with both language practice and homework. There is always a way. If it is what you want to do, you will find a way. You just need to be prepared!

Educación Secundaria Obligatoria (ESO)
State secondary schools (ages 12 to 16 years)
Bachillerato (ages 16 to 19 years)

This secondary stage of education is compulsory and also free.

It comprises of 4 courses divided into 2 cycles of 2 years each. The first cycle is for pupils from 12 to 14 years and the second from 14 to 16 years.

On successfully completing this education stage, pupils are awarded the certificate of Secondary Education Graduate giving access to Bachillerato and medium-grade training cycles in Spanish schools.

All towns and cities have secondary schools which are generally known as Institutos.

If your child is not fluent in Spanish, please seriously rethink about placing them in education at this late stage.

Like primary schools, some secondary schools teach subjects in the regional dialect rather than in Spanish. This can create problems as it will mean that your child will have to learn two languages simultaneously whilst also undertaking increasingly difficult academic work.

Obviously, you must research secondary schooling with the same rigour that you would apply in the UK or your own country. At the best of times, this can be a difficult process with personal recommendations being the best way of finding out the real truth about a given school.

Local estate agents tend to be sensitive to local schools particularly if they have children of their own in the educational system. Indeed, there is probably no better proof than another parent of your own nationality being happy with the local schooling of their own child.

Entry to a secondary school also depends upon the catchment area in which you live.

At the age of 16 a child should attain a Certificate of Completion of Secondary Education (Titulo de Graduado en Educación Secundaria) if they have successfully passed their examinations (examen or control).

If they have not been successful then they will leave school with a Certificado de Escolarización. If a child has achieved their Titulo de Graduado en Educacion Secundaria then they can decide to:

- Leave school
- Continue their education by studying for the Bachillerato (essential for university)
- Continue to attend their school by taking a vocational course (Ciclo Formativo)

Researching Information about Spanish schools

Information about Spanish schools, state and private, can be obtained from Spanish embassies and consulates abroad, and from foreign embassies, educational organisations and government departments in Spain. Information about local schools can be obtained from town halls (ayuntamientos).

The Ministry of Education and Science (Ministerio de Educación y Ciencia) provides a general information service at its central office (Servicio de Información, C/Alcalá, 36, 28071 Madrid, 902-218 500, http://www.mec.es).

The autonomous regions also have their own education offices in regional capitals.

A Google search for the area you are considering will usually bring up the names of schools and the different education options.

I am happy to help you with this, if needed, but I will never tell you which school to select.

I believe this is a decision that only you should make.

Enrolment Procedures

Initial applications for new students take place in March each year. There are a series of official forms that must be completed and submitted from March 1st to 31st.

You can obtain the forms from your school of choice or download them from this website: http://www.juntadeandalucia.es/educacion/webportal/web/portal-escolarizacion/infantil-primaria-eso-bachillerato/impresos

The application form for infantil, primaria and ESO can be downloaded from this website http://housesforsaleinmijas.com/wp-content/uploads/2014/03/educacion-primaria-application-form.pdf

One of the most important requirements when submitting the applications is that you are registered on the Padrón (the electoral role at the local town hall).

I will explain this later in the NIE & Residency section. Secondly, you must show the copy of the birth certificate where the parents are named. Failure to demonstrate parenthood will result in an application being rejected.

On the initial application you can select up to three schools in order of preference.

Be advised that certain factors are taken into consideration when allocating places. These include: the location of the family home, other siblings already enrolled in the school etc. Hence the importance of researching schools prior to selecting properties to rent or purchase!

In the first week of June, the list of students accepted in each school is published.

The application process to the particular school must then be completed. This involves completing authorisation forms, applying for after school activities, canteen services etc. This is carried out at your allocated school.

If you are unable to time your move to coincide with the start of a new school year, it is essential that you check availability in schools before deciding on a property. Many schools are oversubscribed and will not be able to offer your child a place. Again, please do your research!

School Term Times

The academic year in Spain is quite similar to the English three term system, but with slightly shorter holidays at Christmas, which run from as late as December 23rd until January 8th (after King's Day ...Los Reyes Magos) and Easter which is only one week at "Semana Santa". Not forgetting the long summer holidays which start around June 23rd until about September 15th, depending on the regions.

The English half-term holidays do not exist, but there are also frequent odd days and long weekends relating mainly to religious holidays and regional and national holidays.

We publish the school calendar each year on our website www.familylifeinspain.com.

Finding the Best Schools in Malaga

The region of Málaga is one of the most popular destinations for people, of all nationalities, relocating to Spain.

Thanks to its excellent transportation network, it offers affordable accessibility to most parts of the world on most days of the week.

Famous for its wonderful climate and outdoor Mediterranean diet and lifestyle, the Málaga region is a favourite amongst families looking for a new life abroad. Read this great post "A to Z Reasons to live in Malaga" http://movetomalagaspain.com/a-to-z-reasons-to-live-in-malaga/

Due to the cosmopolitan nature of this part of Spain, there is a wide range of education options available to children of all ages and all nationalities.

There are many International Schools in Malaga to choose from. Some of these International Schools follow the British System but are not regulated by OFSTED. They are monitored and regulated by the Junta de Andalucía Consejería de Educación (Junta de Andalucía Education Department).

All British Schools in Spain are inspected by the local authorities before being issued with a licence to operate as a school for foreigners. The Curriculum is monitored by the British Council who ensures that the correct curriculum is followed and that teachers have the correct UK recognised qualifications.

An official B.O.J.A. (Boletin official de la Junta de Andalucía) is issued by the Junta de Andalucía once the school has been approved. This licence should be clearly displayed within the school.

There are many towns offering education at International Schools in Malaga and a high percentage of them in the Marbella area and consequently fees in this area tend to be higher, however higher fees are not a reflection of higher standards.

State Schools in Malaga

If you have decided that you would rather send your children to one of the state Schools in Malaga rather than a private or international school, you may wish to check out the Junta de Andalucía's website.

It provides a concise list of state schools in Malaga and all provinces of Andalucía.

Although only in Spanish, the website is relatively self-explanatory. By inputting the post code or the village/town where you are planning to move to, you can see the schools in that area.

See the Junta de Andalucia list of education centres HERE (http://www.juntadeandalucia.es/educacion/vscripts/centros/)

Please note than in Andalucía, the state school timetable for lessons is generally from 9am until 2pm.

In most schools, there is a canteen option (*Comedor) at extra cost, extra-curricular activities (*Actividades Extrascolares), at extra cost and an early morning drop off option (*Aula Matinal) at extra cost.

NOTE: It is important to check these details as they will influence not only your daily life but also the location of your new home. A 30 minute school run, four times a day, soon eats into your precious free time!

Resources to Help You

National Association of British Schools in Spain (http://nabss.org/) which is a membership organisation comprising of only fully authorised British schools and which is a fabulous site if you're planning on putting your children through a private, British school.

All the schools are listed with contact details, an overview of the school and the age ranges accepted.

British Council in Spain's (http://www.britishcouncil.org/spain/) website that has plenty of resources for parents as well as their student children.

Extra Notes

• The Spanish way of teaching can vary from older, traditional British ways. As parents, you took will be learning new methods and techniques. For example, read my post on division (http://familylifeinspain.com/education-in-spain-division/) Keep an open mind, be prepared to go back to school yourself and enjoy the ride.

• Academic Diplomas: Research your options for higher education, allowing yourself plenty of time, as individual governments of EU countries remain responsible for their education systems and are free to apply their own rules, including whether or not to recognise academic qualifications obtained in other countries. In most cases, you can obtain a "statement of comparability" of your university degree, stating how it compares to the diplomas delivered in the EU country you are moving to. Further reading here: http://www.mecd.gob.es/portada-mecd/en/

Education: Our Story

The following three articles are taken from our website. They share our journey, the rough with the smooth, as our children adapt to their new Spanish school …

Part One

In our post Education in Spain (part 1), we mentioned that probably, the first decision you have, regarding your child's education, when moving to Spain is the choice to place them in a state run school or a private / International school.

In one sense, our decision making process was made more simple by the fact that both our children were born in Spain (Fuerteventura, Canary Islands), and have never lived in the UK. It is generally considered that the younger a child is, entering the Spanish education system, the better they cope.

This is not however a guarantee; the child's character, ability and individual needs must also be taken into consideration. What was for us, in comparison, a "piece of cake" transition with our son, was a real shock to the system with our daughter.

Our son attended a private Spanish nursery part time from the age of 12 months. At age 3 he attended a French state school (during our very short attempt at "Family Life In France"!), from age 4 he attended a state school near Velez-Malaga. Aged 5, he moved to Spanish state school in Mijas pueblo where, this year (2010) he has moved up into 1st year Primary (primer ciclo de educación primaria). No doubt, some of you will be shaking your head, wondering how a child could cope with such change in his early years … I know I am his mother, but I can proudly say that he is one of the most contented, responsible and well adapted little boys I know. His school reports are the kind every caring mother hopes to receive. At aged, almost 6, he is completely bilingual, he has an in depth understanding of both the UK and Spanish culture and a thirst for more.

Tip: Many state Spanish schools offer a Summer School (escuela de verano) in July and August. This is a great way for your child to get to know some of their new classmates before the start of the new school year in September. If you are unable to check details direct with the school, try asking for information at your local social services office.

Part Two

The experience with our daughter was not so smooth ...

In our previous post Education in Spain (Our Story I), we told of how smoothly our eldest son adapted to changes.

Our daughter however, appears to have suffered more due to the changes in her young life.

At the age of 15 months, she eventually adapted to private Spanish nursery in Velez-Malaga. An attempt to start the Spanish state nursery in Mijas pueblo, 10 months later, ended after 2 weeks of non-stop tears and an unrecognisable little girl!

In no way do I mean to criticise the Spanish state nurseries, however, the noise levels and general mayhem on entering and leaving the establishment made my decision to go elsewhere a very easy one.

As I mentioned earlier, each child's needs are very different and we recognised our daughter's need for a more quiet and controlled environment.

On recommendation from a friend, she started a private bilingual nursery in Fuengirola and, much to our relief, by day 2 she was walking in happily ... at last, we had our happy little girl back!

In September 2010, she started the state school in Mijas pueblo. During the parents' pre term meeting we were given the option to have an adaptation period (periódo de adaptacón). This entailed the children attending school for half an hour, for a couple of days and gradually working up to the full 5 hours ... this used to be obligatory for new pupils, however, this year the teacher advised us that, although strongly recommended, she was not allowed to enforce it.

To my horror, only 5 of the 23 pupils in our daughter's class choose the adaptation period. Can you imagine the chaos of twenty-three little 3 year olds from 9am to 2pm on the first days? Not surprisingly, our daughter did not have much fun …

The weeks that followed saw her being dragged, screaming, from us by one or two staff members, many of whom received punches and kicks to various parts of their bodies. "Distraught & devastated" does not even get near to describing our emotions every morning . We were "those" parents of "that" child! As hard as it was, we stuck to our guns and followed the advice of others and persevered.

After what seemed like an eternity, but was only two months later, she is loving school and is singing and dancing and babbling way (in her own lovely way) in Spanish.

Part Three

Eventually, I finally got to meet our daughter's new teacher, Marie Tere.

Time had flown and Francesca was now in Primaria (aged 6 years old).

This is the start of the compulsory stage of education in Spain.

Generally, at our school in Mijas, CEIP San Sebastian, we have a parents meeting at the beginning of every trimester.

The aim of the meeting is for the teacher to explain the subjects and topics to be covered in the coming months and also to discuss the general progress of the students.

My first impression of Marie Tere was ... "she smiles as she talks"!

I can see why Francesca was so happy with her. It was also very comforting to be told by other parents that Francesca seemed so much happier at school this year.

The tears were less frequent.

The confidence was building ... but, we knew, the insecurity was still a big, scary monster in her beautiful, little head.

My second feeling was that of passion and enthusiasm.

Marie Tere oozed excitement as she talked about the topics they would be covering, the innovative methods that they would be using. The text books will take a back seat in all this. Interaction is the principal focus. Stimulating their young minds and encouraging a yearn for learning is the main goal. I was a happy bunny!

Then she started taking about Regletas ... what?

According to Wikipedia: Cuisenaire rods give students a hands-on elementary school way to learn elementary maths concepts, such as the four basic arithmetical operations and working with fractions.

In the early 1950s, Caleb Gattegno popularised this set of coloured number rods created by the Belgian primary school teacher Georges Cuisenaire (1891-1976), who called the rods réglettes.

The educationalists Maria Montessori and Friedrich Fröbel had used rods to represent numbers, but it was Cuisenaire who introduced their use to teachers across the world from the 1950s onwards.

He published a book on their use in 1952 called Les nombres en couleurs.

Cuisenaire, a violin player, taught music as well as arithmetic in the primary school in Thuin.

He wondered why children found it easy and enjoyable to pick up a tune and yet found mathematics neither easy nor enjoyable.

These comparisons with music and its representation led Cuisenaire to experiment in 1931 with a set of ten rods sawn out of wood, with lengths from 1 cm to 10 cm.

He painted each length of rod a different colour and began to use these in his teaching of arithmetic.

The invention remained almost unknown outside the village of Thuin for about 23 years, until Gattegno came to visit him and observe lessons in 1953.

With Gattegno's help, the use of the rods for both mathematics and language teaching was developed and popularised in many countries around the world.

According to Gattegno,

"Georges Cuisenaire showed in the early fifties that students who had been taught traditionally, and were rated 'weak', took huge strides when they shifted to using the (Cuisenaire) material. They became 'very good' at traditional arithmetic when they were allowed to manipulate the rods."

Las Regletas de Cuisenaire (Cuisenaire rods) are basically mathematical material intended for children to learn the composition and decomposition of numbers and their introduction to computing activities, via manipulation The material consists of a set of wooden blocks of ten sizes and colours.

The length of the blocks ranges from 1 to 10 cm.

Each block corresponds to a specific number :

    The white strip of 1 cm length represents the number 1.

    The red strip of 2 cm represents the number 2 .

    The light green strip of 3 cm represents the number three .

    The pink strip of 4 cm represents the number 4.

    The yellow strip of 5 cm represents the number 5 .

    The dark green strip of 6 cm represents the number 6.

    The black strip of 7 cm represents the number 7.

    The brown strip of 8 cm represents the number 8.

    The blue strip of 9 cm represents the number 9.

    The orange strip of 10 cm represents the number 10 .

At this point, I must admit to having a mix of emotions. All this talk of exciting and innovative teaching methods and then resorting to what we would probably call "counting blocks". But I remained optimistic and looked forward to learning and experimenting with this new (to myself!) method.

I left the classroom feeling happy and excited at this new stage in our daughter's life in Spain. Every day she woke up and was excited to go to school … I am still very grateful and feel that we made progress!

ONWARDS AND UPWARDS … CUISENAIRE RODS AND ALL!

Remember that you can follow our children's progress and read lots of other education related posts on our website www.familylifeinspain.com under the "Education" category.

Healthcare

"Sometimes Private Medical Healthcare is the easiest option, at least in the short run."

The Spanish Healthcare System
What are You Entitled to?

Both my children were born in a Spanish state hospital and have been cared for by the state health service throughout their young lives. I do not have any reason to complain about the service we have received.

We have never felt the need to take out private health insurance. However, we have always contributed to Spanish social security and so have always been entitled to free State Healthcare (although there have been challenges … more to follow later!).

But, times have changed. Money is tighter than before. Access to healthcare in Spain is not as straight forward as it used to be. You will need to learn how to work your way around the bureaucratic maze.

Things changed with the new law, of April 2012 (RD-ley 16/2012 de asistencia sanitaria). Before this, any EU citizen could register as a resident, and after this you would get your social security, but things have changed. We understand that these laws were introduced to discourage "medical tourism".

So, who is entitled to Spanish healthcare assistance according to the new law? ("prestación sanataria" is the correct term in Spanish)

If you become a Spanish resident after 24th April 2012 and one of the following:

- You are working as self-employed or you have a Spanish work contract.
- You have a S1 from your home country: the S1 shows that your home country is transferring your medical assistance to Spain (they will pay for healthcare). The S1 is personal, they will do one for each family member, even if you depend on a person with a pension and have not have one yourself.
- You have private healthcare insurance
- You are a Dependant/beneficiary (see below for requirements)

If you were a resident before 24th April 2012, according to the new law you are entitled to healthcare if you:

- Qualify for the "low means scheme"
- Were a resident from before 24th April 2012
- You do not receiving health coverage in your home country. (Your country writes you a letter, it's called legislative letter)
- Earn less than 100.000,00 euros/year (one hundred thousand)
- Are working as self-employed or you have a Spanish work contract.
- Have a S1 from your home country: the S1 shows that your home country is transferring your medical assistance to Spain. Being someone's Dependant / beneficiary (see below for requirements)
- Are claiming unemployment benefit ("paro"), the INEM pays for your social security. IMPORTANT NOTE: if you stop receiving the benefit and you stop being a "demandante de empleo", (a job seeker), you will LOSE your healthcare in 90 days, BUT if you continue to be registered as one you will continue to receive it.

Note: The S1 given by the U.K. does have a limited period of coverage usually 2.5 years maximum. (This is currently undergoing changes, ensure you speak with a specialist at the DHS)

Not only EU countries transfer benefits, there are other countries that have special agreements with Spain, so when in doubt ask at the instituto nacional de la seguridad social (INSS) (details at the end of this chapter)

UK: To apply for the legislative letter you must contact the Overseas Healthcare Team, Dept. of Works & Pensions (DWP), Tyne View Park, Newcastle upon Tyne NE98 1BA (Tel. 0191 218 1999). For State Pension 44 191 21 87777

When it has been recognised that you are entitled to Spanish healthcare assistance, your dependants can also be covered.

Who can be a "Dependant"?

- Husband/wife,
- "Pareja de hecho" (common law partners this has to be registered as such)
- Offspring until the age of 26 years. If 26 years or over they must have equal or more than 65% of disability.
- Ex-husband/wife, as long as you receive an income from them (other than child benefit: it is called a "pension compensatoria")

What happens when the S1 expires or you stop working or you are no longer a Dependant? What are your options?

1. Resident before 24th April 2012: (low means scheme)
2. Resident from 24th April 2012:
   a. Private insurance
   b. Someone's dependant
   c. work

d. Government scheme: you can "buy into " the prestación sanitaria (rd 576/2013) it's called "convenio especial para asistencia sanitaria" and these are the requirements:

1. Empadronamiento.
2. Must have been resident for at least ONE year.
3. Pay 60€ per month if under 65 yrs or 157€ per month if 65 years or over.

This scheme is not working seamlessly in every autonomous community. It works in Valencia, Galicia, Castilla y León and Murcia. (Contact http://compasshealthcareguidance.com/ for more details and assistance).

To get your entitlement to healthcare recognised, you need to go to the INSS (instituto nacional de la seguridad social). Offices usually need pre booked appointments that can be made via the internet or by telephone.

To get the "convenio especial" you need to go to the Tesoreria de la seguridad social office that is nearest to you (not the INSS!), and ask for the scheme in royal decree 576/2013 (convenio especial para asistencia sanitaria): beware that many official's don't even know this exists! So, be prepared to show or tell them the legislation, they might tell you that this is only for people that are returning to Spain, THIS IS WRONG, they just have not been informed of this as it only began to function in Oct 2013. It is not running smoothly in Andalucía, but it has been done is some offices.

EHIC - (European Healthcare Insurance Card)

The better-known E111 health card was replaced by the EHIC (European Health Insurance Card) in January 2006. The current EHIC card allows you to receive emergency treatment when you visiting other European countries and as such can be used temporarily in Spain, however it cannot be used to provide continuing treatment or if you are a permanent resident in Spain.

Please note that if you have children, then they will also need to be included in your application with each member your family receiving their own EHIC card. All EHIC cards are valid for 5 years and at which time will need to be renewed.

Application forms are available from the NHS website, more information here:

http://www.nhs.uk/nhsengland/healthcareabroad/ehic/pages/about-the-ehic.aspx

Application forms are available from the NHS website, more information here:

http://www.nhs.uk/nhsengland/healthcareabroad/ehic/pages/about-the-ehic.aspx

You can also apply for a EHIC card by obtaining a form at your local Post Office branch: http://www.postoffice.co.uk/health-insurance-card or by calling the NHS directly on 0845 606 2030

Please Note that once you apply for Spanish residency, your EHIC entitlements become invalid. If applicable you will need to apply for the Spanish equivalent. (Read about the Tarjeta Sanitaria Europea later in this chapter).

A campaign to explain how British citizens in Spain should use UK-issued European Health Insurance Cards (EHICs) has been launched by the UK Department of Health and the Valencia Health Authority.

The EHIC Campaign aims to greatly raise awareness among British citizens and Spanish healthcare staff in the Valencia Autonomous Community over the next 15 months. The innovative partnership between a UK government department and a Spanish regional authority has been recognised by the European Union, which is funding the campaign.

What you should know about the UK European Health Insurance Card

The UK European Health Insurance Card should only be used to access medically-necessary state treatment during the course of a temporary stay in Spain. It provides all of the necessary state treatment but for those in Spain on a temporary stay, it is the correct way to access state healthcare.

However British citizens who live mainly in Spain should change the way they are registered, because for them the UK European Health Insurance Card is not the correct form of health cover. The new EHIC marketing and advertising campaign will explain how to do this. More details can be found on www.healthcareinspain.eu.

Private Health Insurance in Spain

Sometimes Private Medical Healthcare is the easiest option, at least in the short run. Many people choose to take out a private healthcare policy when they first move to Spain and until they are settled and have all the necessary paperwork in place to apply for Spanish healthcare cover.

Although the Spanish healthcare service has an excellent reputation, it is not uncommon to have doctors who do not speak English. It is important to consider this when first moving to Spain. The frustration of not being able to communicate with a doctor attending to a family member, particularly a child, can be unbearable. Opting for private insurance, at least until you are familiar with the systems and also the language is a sensible option that need not be too expensive.

Choosing the best insurance in Spain for you and your family is not always as easy as in your home country. Most companies and websites only offer their own insurance policies. Insurance brokers are not a common as in other countries. This can make searching for insurance in Spain quite a tedious task.

Using an independent insurance broker who offers all kinds of insurance policies for health cover, home and contents, vehicles, pets and much more, with policies from over twenty different insurance companies is a good option.

As an independent broker, they do the work for you, searching for the best policy for your insurance in Spain, whatever type it may be and for the policy that best suits your needs.

What you need to be aware of private insurance is that there is a lot of small print, so you may find yourself paying for 25 years, and then the treatment you need is not covered. Always ask specific questions before signing up for cover.

Who should take out Health Insurance in Spain?

Anybody who has not been a resident in Spain since 2012 and is not contributing to the Spanish social security system, either as an employee on a Spanish contract (receiving a nomina) or a self-employed worker (autonomo)*.

(*Please note this does not include pensioners who have reciprocal agreements within member states!)

Most expats take out private medical insurance in Spain, not just for medical care, but also for ambulance and dental services. If you are not covered by the Spanish social security healthcare system, it would be wise to take insurance sooner rather than later, so that you do not risk being uninsurable for medical problems which arise over the course of time and to avoid any unexpected and expensive medical bills.

The Spanish equivalent of the European Health Insurance Card (EHIC) is the Tarjeta Sanitaria Europea (TSE).

If you are resident in Spain, have a Spanish social security number (Nº afiliación S.S.) and you are paying your contributions into the Spanish Social Security system, you should apply for this card.

If you are traveling back to the UK, or to any other European country, on holiday, on business or to visit family and friends and require medical assistance, presentation of the Tarjeta Sanitaria Europea will entitle you to receive medical assistance, free of charge.

Please be advised, however, that this does not entitle you to travel to a country specifically to receive medical treatment.

You can apply for the card online at http://costaconsultingbureau.com/spanish-paperwork/european-health-insurance-card-in-spain/ or alternatively visit your nearest social security office.

Being a British passport holder no longer entitles you to free healthcare in the UK. Failure to present your European Health

Insurance Card may result in you receiving a bill for any medical treatment received.

In Malaga we are very lucky to have the services of Compass Healthcare Guidance TM.

As a consequence of the difficulties expats are having with the Spanish NHS, a new service of patient advocacy called Compass Healthcare Guidance TM has started to operate in the Malaga area and the Costa del Sol. This is the only one of its kind, in Spain. Managed by a Physician and veteran of the public healthcare of Andalucía and the private system, she help patients & provides guidance in the bureaucratic and medical sides of the system.

Being ill is a time when you should not be worrying about if the appointment arrives, or if you understand your doctor's answers. It is a time to concentrate in your improvement. Sadly that can very difficult to do if you do not speak the language, it is difficult even if you do!

A physician patient advocate like Dr. Tacchi helps in explaining the medicine, helping to take decisions and tackling with the bureaucracy.

She writes a blog updating news & insider tips on the Spanish NHS at http://compasshealthcareguidance.com/

She offers face to face treatment with patients from Malaga Capital to Sabanillas/ Manilva, and distance sessions via Skype or telephone, to guide you to the best pathway available.

Useful Contacts in Spain

Instituto Nacional de la Seguridad Social (INSS). This is the Spanish authority that deals with all applications for pensions, benefits and access to healthcare. Each province has a 'Dirección Provincial', which will deal with any application that involves another EU Member State. There are also smaller offices across Spain, which are called 'Centros de Atención e Información'

(CAISS), where customers can go to register for access to healthcare and to collect or hand in application forms. Tel: 900 166 565 Website: www.seg-social.es

Tesorería General de la Seguridad Social (TGSS). This is the equivalent of the UK HMRC although they only deal with social security contributions, not tax. Customers will only need to contact the TGSS if they wish to get a social security number in order to be able to work in Spain, or if they wish to make voluntary contributions and pay as an 'autónomo'. Each province also has a 'Dirección Provincial' along with smaller offices called 'Administraciones'.
Tel: 901 502 050 Website: www.seg-social.es

Useful Contacts in the UK

International Pension Centre (IPC). The IPC issues the S1 form to UK State Pension and long-term Sickness Benefit recipients who are living abroad. Tel: (+44) 191 218 7777
Website: www.gov.uk/international-pension-centre

Overseas Healthcare Team (OHT) The OHT issues the S1 form to people who have contributed to the UK National Insurance Scheme in the last 3 years but no longer work. This form is valid for up to 2.5 years. The OHT also issues EHIC application forms to registered S1 holders and Provisional Replacement Certificates in the case of a lost EHIC. Tel: (+44) 191 218 1999 Website: www.gov.uk/dh

Her Majesty's Revenue & Customs (HMRC) HMRC issues the S1 form to workers and their families who are posted abroad within the European Union and who continue to make national insurance contributions in the UK. Tel: (+44) 191 203 7010
Website: www.gov.uk/hmrc

NOTE: I would like to thank Dr. Tacchi from Compass Healthcare Guidance for checking the information included in this chapter and for providing an excellent and often needed service for many people who move to Spain. Do not hesitate to contact her with your questions, via her website http://compasshealthcareguidance.com/

NIE & Residency

"The application procedures for both NIE and Residency are quite simple. It is often not necessary to pay expensive lawyer's fees."

NIE, Residency & The Padrón

There is a lot of confusing and conflictive information published on websites and forums regarding NIE and Residency application requirements and procedures.

When moving to Spain, your NIE or Residency application should be at the top of your "To Do" list.

Procedures are changing regularly so it is important to keep updated with the changes.

The application procedures for both NIE and Residency are quite simple. It is often not necessary to pay expensive lawyer's fees. You can submit your own applications by following the instructions given in the following pages.

What is a NIE Number and Do I Need One?

An NIE number is a "Número de Identificación de Extranjero" i.e. a "foreigner's identification number" in Spain.

If you wish to purchase a property, open a bank account, buy a car, set up a mobile phone contract in Spain, you will require an NIE.

An NIE number is also required to work in Spain, take out private Spanish health insurance and apply for Spanish state health cover.

The Decree (Real Decreto 338-1990) March 9th, establishes that anyone, of whatever nationality, resident or non-resident, who has any "official business" in Spain, must have a fiscal number (NIF/NIE).

To avoid confusion, if you apply for an NIE only, you will be issued with a white certificate that will assign you your unique foreigner's ID number that is in the format of: A-1234567-Z (i.e. letter-7 digits-letter).

Previously, foreigners arriving in Spain had to firstly apply for an NIE and then later apply for residency. However, rules are often changing and applying for an NIE may not now be the right decision for you.

Subject to your own personal situation you may not need to apply for an NIE. You may be able to save time and money and apply directly for residency.

The following Section will explain how to make that decision.

Should I apply for NIE or Residency?

This is possibly the most frequently asked question on this subject. Yet, the answer is very straightforward.

There is one simple question to ask yourself, which will provide you with the correct answer to this question. That question is, "How long do I intend to stay in Spain?"

If you intend to stay in Spain for more than three months then you should apply directly for Residency, using the EX18 application form (accurate at the time of writing this).

If you plan to stay in Spain for less than three months, then you should apply for a NIE number, using the EX15 application form (accurate at the time of writing this).

The "NIE or Residency?" question is no more complicated than that.

IMPORTANT NOTE: Although using the commonly known term

of "Residency" in our explanations, the new procedure actually results in a "Certificado de Registro de Ciudadano de la UE" which is a Certificate to confirm your inscription in the EU Foreigners Register in Spain.

Applying to be a resident in Spain (as described in this booklet), does not necessarily mean that you are a tax resident in Spain. Whether you become a tax resident in Spain is another matter that should be discussed with an accountant specialised in such matters.

The following pages will guide you through the application procedures.

How to Apply for a NIE

An NIE application is a pretty straight forward procedure as, unlike residency application, no proof of income nor health insurance is required.

However, as the application process may differ slightly in different areas of Spain, it is always a good idea to check out the procedure with your local Police station (Comisaría de Policía) or foreigners department (Departamento de Extranjería). If you are unsure where your local office is, check with your local town hall (Ayuntamiento) or carry out a Google search.

The general steps for NIE application are:

1. Complete the EX15 form. (NOTE: Ensure you print out the form once you have completed it. You cannot save the data.)

2. Take the completed EX15 form with a good, clear copy of your passport and the original. (NOTE: British passport holders must take an additional copy of the front of the passport)

3. Follow the procedures indicated at your local police station.

Please note that some areas issue the NIE certificate immediately but many will ask you to return in 48 to 72 hours.

Since 2012, the NIE certificates are only valid for 3 months, for administrative purposes. ie. A duplicate certificate will need to be requested for legal formalities such as vehicle registration, notarial procedures.

Please note, however, that your personal NIE number will never change.

For step by step instructions how to complete the EX15, please see our Guide to NIE & Residency (RRP €9.99) where we include detailed step by step instructions.

(http://costaconsultingbureau.com/spanish-paperwork-guides/).

How to apply for Residency (for EU citizens)

Since July 2012, the regulations for residency application in Spain have been changed and continue to change. The change in procedures mean that people who apply for residency need to be able to prove that they will not "become a burden on Spain's social assistance during their period of residence". Consequently, the ability to prove financial stability and healthcare cover are very important for a successful residency application. As before, we recommend checking procedures in your area.

The general steps are:

1. Complete the EX18: Spanish Residency Application form (Step by step instructions in the following chapter).

2. Original and copy of applicants valid (ie not expired) passport or national Identity card. In the event that this document has expired, a copy of the expired document and proof of renewal will be required.

3. Bank receipt to declare Spanish Residency Application taxes paid, Modelo 790 (currently 10.50€).

If you are unable to complete this online via the link, you will be issued with a document at the police station.

4. The following documents, subject to the applicant's personal

situation

A. **If the Applicant is employed by a third party** (i.e. with a Spanish work contract), they must submit at least one of the following:

1. A letter from the employer that includes the Name, address and CIF number of the company and the Company's Social Security number (Código Cuenta Cotización en la Seguridad Social).

2. A certificate of employment (including the details stated above).

3. A work contract that has already been presented at the INSS (Instituto Nacional de la Seguridad Social).

4. Proof of registration in the Social Security system (alta en seguridad social).

B. **If the Applicant is self-employed**, they must submit at least one of the following:

1. Proof of inscription in the "Censo de Actividades Económicas" (Modelo 036 or 037).

2. Proof of inscription in the "Registro Mercantil" for a Company.

3. Proof of registration in the Social Security system (alta en seguridad social).

Permission for your details to be checked at the TGSS (Tesorería General de la Seguridad Social) can also be given.

C. **If the Applicant is not working,** all of the following must be submitted:

1. Proof of health insurance for the period of intended stay in Spain (this does not apply to UK pensioners who can provide a copy of their registered E-121* or S-1* forms, *(or the equivalent in other European countries).

2. Proof of sufficient funds, currently a figure of approximately €5,200 per family member, is being stated (Pensioners must prove they are in receipt of regular pension payments).

A bank statement is not always acceptable.

Ask your bank to write a simple "certificado" that includes: Your full name, ID number (e.g. Passport), account number and actual balance on a given date.

D. **If the Applicant is a Student**, there are two possibilities:

1. A course registration document, proof of private health insurance or the EHIC that covers the intended period of residence and a declaration of sufficient funds.

2. Proof of participation in an inter EU educational exchange programme.

Upon completing a successful application, you will be issued with a green residency card/certificate that will include your NIE number. In most places, this is issued on the spot, although regional differences of procedure may exist. At present, this new certificate does not expire. However, procedures and requirements are changed on a regular basis, so it is very important to keep updated with changes in regulations.

We will continue to publish updates on our website as we are informed about them: www.ccbspain.com

As with the NIE application, the residency application process may differ slightly in different areas of Spain so it is always a good idea to check out the procedure with your local Police station (Comisaría de Policía) or foreigners department (Departamento de Extranjería). If you are unsure where your local office is, check with your local town hall (Ayuntamiento) or carry out a Google search.

IMPORTANT: Please note if you are a non EU citizen, you should check visa requirements and procedures with your embassy.

Leaving Spain to return to your Home Country

If you decide to leave Spain and return to your home country or another country, it is advisable to take the following steps:

• inform your Spanish bank: you will need to change your resident account to a non-resident account.

• inform the town hall where you registered and have your name removed from the Padrón (census).

• go to the National Police office where the residency certificate was first issued. They will issue you with a stamped document that includes the date of cancellation and the reason for it.

• If you hold the old style residency card you should return it to the Foreigner's Delegation Office / Police station.

This is your proof that you are no longer a resident and that you have informed the necessary people.

NOTE: These actions will not automatically alter your tax resident status. Please consult your accountant / tax advisor for details of the correct process.

Further updates and information can be consulted via www.ccbspain.com

NOTE: Should you prefer not to carry out these procedures yourself and would like the name of a recommended lawyer to carry out the procedures for you, simply ask me for details.

If you have any questions, queries or even requests for further material, please do not hesitate to contact me via the website or via Skype: Lisa.Sadleir Phoning from the UK: 020 328 96087 and Spanish mobile: 00 34 608 840 692

Registering on the Padrón

Empadronarse is the act of registering yourself on this list with your local town hall.

When you move to a new area in Spain you should register on the Padrón at your local town hall (ayuntamiento), as soon as possible. This is similar to the electoral role, but has much wider usage in Spain than in the UK.

The town council receives a certain amount of government funding for each person registered on the Padrón. This means they have more money to spend on facilities and services, such as roads, libraries, sports facilities, schools, for all its residents.

How You Register

Simply go to the padrón office of your town hall, take along official identification, such as a passport, and also your NIE or residence certificate/card, a recent utility bill in your name (if you have one), and the deeds to your house or a copy of your rental contract.

Ensure you have identification for each family member to be included and that each member is present. This process cannot be carried out by a third party.

Once you are registered on the Padrón you will be able to:

• Register your children at school
• Register with your local medical centre
• Buy a car
• Vote in the local elections (make sure the town hall has your post office box address if you have one, to ensure you receive your voting card)

Please note that if you are buying a car in Spain, a valid Padrón certificate will be required to register the car in your name.

As with most Spanish paperwork, a Padrón certificate is only valid for 3 months after the date of issue. A new certificate is easily issued at your town hall for a small fee.

Registering on the Padrón is a very simple process, provided you have all the paperwork mentioned above. The only real issue that may arise is that if the previous tenants of a rental property have not removed themselves from the Padrón. If this happens, just give me a shout!

NOTE: Rules and regulations are continually changing. To keep unto date with procedures, keep an eye on our website www.ccbspain.com.

NIE & Residency: Our Story

The following extracts are taken from our family blog (www.familylifeinspain.com). Each article was written with view to sharing the trials and tribulations faced when dealing with Spanish bureaucracy. All information provided relates directly to our own personal situation.

I hope these tales help you to realise that it can happen to anyone. Anyone can go to the wrong desk. Anyone can forget a piece of necessary paperwork. Anyone can get the wrong person behind the desk … even me!

WARNING: As I regularly deal with paperwork and Spanish bureaucracy for my clients, I tend to overlook our own bureaucratic needs from time to time. As I result, I am known to get extremely frustrated when things don't go to plan. The following blog posts were written immediately after these events. Please take them with a pinch of salt. Remember, I do want to show you the rough with the smooth!

¿Qué Pasa España?
Residency Application in Spain: ¿Que pasa?

What is going on? Has the Spanish government totally lost the plot or do they have an ulterior motive? What is Spain's future with regard to the eurozone? What is going on with the changes on Residency Application in Spain? As this is not our normal kind of article, you may well be wondering what has caused us to write like this, so let me explain. Recently, we stumbled across an article published on the British Embassy Madrid website. This article was a translation of new residency requirements in Spain as published in the Spanish Order 1490 of 9 July 2012.

The Spanish Order 1490 of 9 July 2012 sets out the rules of entry, free movement and residence in Spain of nationals of other European Union Member States and European Economic Area.

What happened to free movement amongst Member States?

To be honest, I cannot say I disagree with what has been laid down before us but I am also uncertain as how ethical it is, especially if Spain's intention is to remain in the European Union.

In summary, the changes to the conditions for residency application in Spain now require EU nationals to either:

- Produce documentation to prove they have a work contract / certificate of employment accompanied by official social security paperwork or, alternatively, agree to have their employment details checked in the official "Ficheros de la Tesoría General de la Seguridad Social"
- Produce documentation (similar to the above) to prove that they are officially registered as self-employed in Spain
- Non workers must: Have proof of public or private healthcare insurance. Have sufficient resources, for themselves and family members, not to become a burden on Spain's social assistance

system during their period of residence.

What do you think about that? Is it right? Is it wrong?

Many expats in Spain seem to think that Spain is pushing away expats who want to move to Spain. Or are they simply being selective about the type of people they want to allow into their country? I have seen some comments that people think the UK should impose the same measures ...

Recently, changes in procedures for the NIE and Residency application in Spain demonstrated a strong push towards foreigners applying for residency rather than simply obtaining an NIE. Was this to help Spain receive more funding from the EU? If so, then why this reversal in attitude? Surely, any expat in Spain who was thinking about "legalising" their situation in Spain by applying for residency, and not just using their NIE certificate, will now think twice. Have the Spanish government changed their mind? Is EU funding no longer important?

No doubt, more information will become available over the coming weeks and months. In the meantime, how will expats who are already here in Spain be affected?

Please note that, at the end of the original article you will see: *"This Order will apply to applications presented after 24 April 2012"*. *"This Ministerial Order is passed under the provisions of Article 149.1.2 of the Spanish Constitution, which gives States sole jurisdiction in matters of nationality, immigration, foreign affairs and right of asylum" This Order will come into force on the day after its publication in the "State Official Bulletin". (10 July 2012)*

So, basically, the Spanish Government appears to be within their rights imposing these requirements as: "The rules on social security coordination do not replace national systems with a single European one. All countries are free to decide who is to be insured under their legislation, which benefits are granted and under what conditions. The EU provides common rules to protect your social security rights when moving within Europe." Let's see what happened next ...

New Residency in Spain Application Procedure

Rants & A Confession!

A few months ago we informed you about the changes in the Residency in Spain application procedure, in our post entitled ¿Qué pasa España?

Our closing phrase was "Let's see what happens next…"

So, guess what happened next?

At this point, please remember that I earn my living by helping people sort through the maze of Spanish red tape and bureaucracy via our business www.ccbspain.com.

Many an hour is spent battling with authorities on behalf of my wonderful clients.

To people's utter astonishment, I openly admit to loving the challenge and am greatly rewarded by my client's satisfaction.

Last week, I visited the police station in Fuengirola, with two people who had just moved over to Spain and were due to start work, and my husband (Yes… my own husband!) who needed to renew his old style residency card.

We followed the application procedure for the new residencia as detailed in our CCB Spain post Spanish Residency Update and within an hour and a half, which included paying the taxes at the bank (and that involved having to try 3 banks in the nearby area!) and having a coffee, we walked out with two shiny new Spanish Residency Cards.

However, much to our frustration, we had not been able to renew my husband's residency!

Why?

Probably because the immigration officer on the desk was having a bad day!!!

That is how I felt as we walked out of the police station having had to make a new appointment for a completely separate residency application … for somebody who has been a legal resident in Spain for almost 20 years, who owns a house here, whose children are in state school here and who pays a lot of tax here … rant over!

Our new appointment was for Monday 24th September, I say "was" because we were unable to get an appointment at Social Security, for another copy of a piddly piece of paper, to show that his health insurance is covered by my social security payments, until Tuesday 25th!!!

Despite my ranting, we have to admit to we had just not got round to renewing my husband's residency card as we did not need it (That's the confession, by the way).

As a result, we have to start the application procedure all over again as detailed in our article Residency in Spain Renewal Update, we want others to learn from our mistakes and hopefully save them headaches too!

Wait! It wasn't over yet …

To top it all, his passport ran out in October and we were going back to the UK for Christmas that year so we then had to renew his passport and then delay the residency renewal until we had the new passport… and how blumin' expensive are passport renewals these days!

So, the passport renewal applications were ready to be sent off. We would go to the social security office the next week and then we would make another application to renew the residency …hoping that the piddly paper from the Social Security office hadn't expired by then …and people wonder why Spanish paperwork is such a nightmare!

However… It doesn't end there…

Warning! My Husband is an Illegal Immigrant in Spain!
Spain Residency Issues: My Husband's Story

My husband has lived in Spain for over twenty years. We were married in Spain. Our two children were born in Spain. We have a house in Spain. We have a libro de familia. We are fiscal residents in Spain as we declare all our taxes in Spain.

However, he is no longer a resident in Spain and needs to start his application procedure all over again! Why?

We went to the INSS (a branch of the social security office in Spain), to renew a simple printed piece of paper that proves that he is covered by my monthly social security payments. I already hold this piece of paper, but like any other piece of paper in Spain, it is only valid for three months (renewing all these bits of paper keeps a lot of people in work I suppose!), a more recent one is required to apply for his residency.

The appointment was booked via telephone and we were even attended to before our time slot. Good start …. But that was as good as it got!

I explained to the lady sat behind the desk that I needed a new print out of the piece of paper I had, to prove that my husband was covered by my social security contributions for his healthcare in Spain, in order for us to process his residency application.

And her reply was …..

"I'm afraid that I cannot do that."

What? My mouth drops open as I hear the very words that my mind had told me that I was going to hear but I had tried to convince myself that it wouldn't really happen.

Oh, but it did.

"To be named as a beneficiary on your social security, your

husband requires a valid residency certificate."

Now, I need to pause even as I write this. Shock. Horror. Disbelief … She did not really say that did she?

Yes, she did. Even after I had thrown (according to hubby) the libro de familia, proof of last autonomo payment, passports, and whatever other excuse of a piece of paper I could find, across the desk at her … she patiently gave that look that said, "I understand everything you are saying and yes it is ridiculous but that's how it is now"!

As I sat there flabbergasted and asking if I should send my husband back to the UK and what about the children and whatever silly comment I could think of (all the time knowing that it was futile, she was only doing her job and actually, we were in the wrong), she went off to consult with a superior.

Not surprisingly, the reply was that there was nothing they could do. I could not have an updated piece of paper until my husband has a valid residency certificate.

What is the Spanish government playing at? Yes, this is a wonderful place to live for so many reasons, but if they continue to put up barriers to people who want to do things properly, the country will suffer in the long term.

So what's the next step?

In theory, we now have to take out a private medical insurance to enable my husband to apply for the new green residency certificate. Once he has the new certificate, we will make another appointment at the INSS to ensure he is registered as a Dependant on my social security cover for healthcare. After that, well I cannot publish that information now can I?

All because he had the old style residency card that people still say is so much more useful than the current certificate.

However, I much prefer a certificate that does not have an expiry date … or does it? We will see…

Playing the Game of Spanish Bureaucracy

Spanish Bureaucracy: Pick a card, any card .... or maybe chance your luck and roll the dice ... just hope that Lady Luck is on your side (or even better, sat at the desk that attends you).

"The rules of any given game or sport are "theoretically" the same and are written in rule books. A good player keeps up with changes in tactics and ensures they have the required skills to ensure they are at the top of their game.

However, it can be, and often is, argued the outcome of any game is greatly influenced by the referee's interpretation of the given rules.

The same may be said about the never ending debacle of Spanish bureaucracy. In this instance, the referee who will influence the outcome of any given situation is replaced by the person you encounter at the desk, at a particular time of a particular day."

I do not want to dwell on this subject matter too much longer as, if you haven't already read the story so far, you can read it in the previous parts ¿Qué pasa España? , Rants and a Confession, and My Husband is an Illegal Immigrant.

All I want to say is that, having made a quick phone call the previous morning, we walked into the immigration office, again, were attended promptly and efficiently and duly walked out holding my husband's new residencia card. Had we been attended by this person a couple of months previously you would never have read this story.

What did we do differently?

I'm afraid I cannot put that in writing but if you are having troubles yourself, don't hesitate to get in touch and I will be happy to give you some guidelines.

As we said, the rules are the same for everybody, it is the player and the referee that influence the outcome!

Renewing the Padrón Certificate ...a long story!

Confession time (again!). A short time ago, (actually I've just checked and it was twelve months earlier), I wrote a rant about the idiotic bureaucratic system that we often face as residents in Spain.

Twelve months later, I finally cancelled the private insurance policy we were incorrectly forced to take out (to be able to renew my "illegal immigrant" husband's residency status). The next step was to get him registered as one of my dependants on the social security for health cover.

So, we popped up to the pueblo. We are lucky living in Mijas as the Town Hall are extremely friendly and helpful, despite having their hands firmly tied by the infamous red tape of the Spanish bureaucratic system and antiquated procedures.

Rather than walking down the three flights of stairs to where the Padrón certificate issuing department had been the last time I visited, I decided to check at the information desk. Luckily I did as it had changed location, again.

Here is a brief outline of the scene that followed: (translated into English and names added for ease)

Me: *Hi, I'd like an updated copy of our Padrón certificate please*

Maria: *Do you not have access via the online digital system?*

Me: *I'm not sure, how does it work?*

Maria dutifully scribbled some words down on a scrap piece of paper and handed it over to me.

Me: *Can I have a new Padrón certificate now though, as I'm here, I'll try the online system later.*

Maria: *Yes but I'm afraid it will cost you €5 if I issue it and it will be free if you do it online.*

Me: *No problem. I'm happy to pay as I need it now and if I don't do it immediately I will forget again and it will take another few months until I get sorted.*

Maria: Ok, *then you need to go over there to pay, then bring the receipt back to me.*

So, we go over to the first desk only to be advised by Maria to go to the next desk.

Me: *Hi, I'd like to pay for a new Padrón certificate.*

Sonia: *Can I have a passport please?*

Me: *Is the new Padrón certificate for all the family or just one person?*

Sonia: *Oh, I can't answer that. You'll have to go back to the other desk and ask Maria.*

Me: *Oh, don't worry. Just put it in my husband's name then.*

Sonia: *That's five euros please. Are you paying with credit card?*

Me: *No, I'll pay cash thanks.*

Sonia: *Ok, then you'll have to go and pay at the bank and bring me the receipt to issue you a receipt to take back to Maria.*

Me: *Ok, I'll pay by card then.*

I hand over my bank card to Sonia who nudges her colleague to ask her if she can process the payment, colleague grunts, staples a few more bits of paper. She asks Maria to give her the reference number which she duly types into her computer. She hands me the credit card machine to input my PIN. The receipt is printed and stapled to the invoice and handed to me. I thank them both politely and head back towards Maria's desk.

By this time there is quite a queue at Maria's desk. Hubby, (typically British in his politeness), heads to the back of the queue. I catch Maria's eye, give her a smile and slip to the front of the queue. Before anyone has the time to notice, Maria is efficiently printing, logging and stamping our new Padrón certificate.

I thank her politely for her friendly efficient service and wish her and her colleagues a lovely day.

I nudge hubby and walk out of the Town Hall, new Padrón certificate in hand.

I will however be looking into using the online digital system in the future and will share my findings with you.

It is true to say that procedures are changing in Spain but at a donkey's pace … the Burro will feature strongly in Spanish "burrocracia" for a few years to come. Just remember to be patient, be polite and give them a smile.

I'm sure many of you who already live in Spain can no doubt relate to this scenario. For those of you thinking about moving to Spain, just remember that the secret to successfully relocating to Spain is to bring your sense of humour with you and be prepared, typically by learning as much as you can beforehand and not stressing when things do not get done immediately. There's always "Mañana" …

Starting a Business

"Setting up a company in Spain is harder than in Zambia" ... or so the newspapers will have you believe!

Starting a Business in Spain

Unemployment in Spain, as in many other countries, is currently at one of its highest ever levels. Finding work in Spain, especially if you do not speak Spanish, is a lot harder than back in the UK. As I have continually stressed, I would not advise moving to Spain unless you have a guaranteed source of income.

You are not entitled to unemployment benefit in Spain until you have been working, and most importantly, making social security contributions over a minimum period of 360 days within the last 6 years before you became unemployed.

A popular option for many expats in Spain, and maybe even for you, is to start your own business. What? How? Why? I hear you asking ... but this idea may not be as crazy as it first appears.

Do you have an original concept? Have you noticed a gap in the market that could be filled by your concept? Do you have some basic funding to start up? If so, what have you got to lose?

It has been seen that many businesses that start up and survive when times are tough, go on to flourish and expand as the economic climate improves.

The bureaucratic procedures in Spain can be challenging, to say the least, but if you plan and prepare and use to services of a professional, you will find your way around the maze. Financial awareness is key. Unlike in the UK, you are liable for taxes and contributions, irrelevant of your income. A good assessor (business advisor and accountant) is the key to your success in this area.

Starting a Business in Spain

If you are thinking of starting a business in Spain, you will probably be deciding between starting up as self-employed (autonomo) or creating a Limited Compamy (Sociedad Limitada, SL) as these are the most common options.

Possibly, the easiest and most cost effective way of setting up a business in Spain is to register as autonomo (self-employed) .

To register as Self-Employed in Spain

1. Go to your local social security office with your NIE (Número de Identidad/Identificación de Extranjeor) and passport to obtain your social security number NAF (Numero de afiliación a la Seguridad Social).

2. Once you have your social security number (NAF), take this to the Agencia Tributaria and ask for a Modelo 036 or 037 to register the activity for your new business. Here is a list of autonomo category codes (http://familylifeinspain.com/autonomo-category-codes/) you can choose from. Ensure you choose the right activity for your new business as this will decide the level of business tax IAE (Impuesto sobre Actividades Econimicas) you will be subject to.

3. Return to the social security office with your bank book to set up the monthly social security payments.

How much will it cost? The biggest cost of being self-employed in Spain is the social security payments that are approximately €250 per month. In some circumstances this amount can be reduced.

There has been a recent promotion, to encourage new business creation, that entitles some people to heavily reduced rates of social security payments, from as little as €50 per month. Please consult the current rates with a reliable gestor or assessor.

Accountant fees for submitting the correct quarterly and annual VAT returns and tax reports can cost anything from €65 up to €150 per month. You are also responsible for advance income tax payments IRPF (Reglamento del Impuesto sobre la Renta de las Personas Físicas). These are paid on a quarterly basis and on presentation of your Annual tax report (Declaración de la Renta) you may be entitled to a tax rebate.

Setting up a Limited Company

Previously, many people started as autonomo and eventually progressed to an SL. The main reason for this was the high cost of starting an SL and the accounting expenses associated with the SL.

The expensive option of starting a business in Spain as an SL is no longer expensive.

CCB Spain are pleased to announce a new "Express SL" (Sociedad Limitada) Service for starting a business in Spain.

So, how do you start an SL in Spain with the help of CCB Spain?

The following are a brief summary of the steps we will take you through.

1. Choose a company name. This will be the official name for the SL but does not necessarily need to be the operating / promotional name. Submit 5 choices of name, in order of preference.

A name must be unique and must not resemble a name that has already been registered.

Note: Names containing only one word are often rejected.

2. Option to Trademark the company Name* Upon acceptance of a name, you have the option to protect the name. ie. Trademark. (*please note this is an additional cost)

3. **Injection of Capital** To constitute the SL, you are required to inject capital, to the value of €3000, into the business. This can be in the form of cash paid into a bank account which is frozen until the SL is fully registered and functional or in the form of an "aportacion no dinerario" which can include items such as computers, office furniture or vehicles.

4. **Preparation of Company Deeds** Once the injection of capital has been documented, the next step is to visit the notary to prepare the Company deeds (escritura). At this point, you must be clear who will be listed as the Company administrator/s and shareholders and how the shares will be divided. There can be as many shareholders as desired however it is advisable to limit administrators to one (unipersonal) or two people (solidario o mancomunado). The Company's activities must also be listed in the deeds. Our business advisor will assist you with this, as CHANGES are very COSTLY!

NOTE: The administrator is required to be registered and contributing to the social security system.

5. **The Notary** Once the deeds have been signed by the administrator(s) and shareholders, the notary will register the Company with the tax office (Hacienda), acquire the Company's Tax number (CIF) and register the Company with the Spanish equivalent of company's House (Registro Mercantil).

6. **Accounting and Reporting Obligations** Our CCB Spain accountants will advise you on a personal basis regarding the day to day obligations of your new SL. With our attention to detail and excellent customer service, you can rest assured that everything will be taken care of for you.

Some important points to remember

• The Spanish tax office (Hacienda) does not send notifications via the post. Hence, it is vital to obtain a Certificado Digital for the Company. This allows you to access the notifications published on the Hacienda's website.

• It is advisable to check for notifications at least every 10 days. For example, if you are required to present any documentation at Hacienda, you will be notified via the website. If you miss the date you are likely to receive a fine. You cannot claim that you were not advised. It is your (or your assessor's) duty to check this information!

• It is essential that the accounting procedures are adhered to and accounts and reports submitted on time to avoid costly penalties.

• Subject to how many "employees" you have, there are different contract options available to you. Our business advisor (assessor) will advise you about this on an individual basis.

So, how much does it cost to set this up?

Previously, set up costs have amounted to 2000 to 3000€ euros plus monthly accounting fees of around €250.

Our new CCB Spain "Express SL Set Up and Accounts Management" costs from only €750* (plus notary fees)

Accounting Packages: from only €115* per month

(*all prices exclude IVA) (**SL Set Up at reduced rate available only with minimum 12 month accounting package)

So, if you are thinking of setting up a business in Spain, contact us now.

Buying Property

"Do your homework and take your time. Mistakes are expensive. Get it right first time. You will know when the time is right."

Buying a Property in Spain

I have said it many times already and I will say it again here. Do not rush into buying a property in Spain. Do not be pushed by an eager sales agent who is offering you the opportunity of a lifetime. Do your homework and take your time. Mistakes are very expensive. Get it right first time. You will know when the time is right.

Now that I have stated my case again, I would like to share some invaluable information with you that will help you avoid any problems when the time arrives that you are ready to purchase a property in Spain.

It may now surprise you to read that I collaborate with a property finding company and have helped many people successfully purchase property in Spain. As you have hopefully realised by now, we are not the pushy sales type. We want what is best for our clients.

Buying property in Spain can be a complicated and stressful process. The tabloids are full of negative stories about foreigners who have lost their savings on property abroad. However, every year, thousands of foreigners buy property in Spain. Many of these purchasers are very happy... but the tabloids don't talk about them, do they!

The following information will give you some insider information to buying property in Spain, provided by the Spanish Property Network:

The Complicated Maze of Property Sales in Spain

Due to the high number of estate agents in Spain, it is common practice for agents to share properties. This basically means that you will very often find the same property advertised on several websites, often at different prices and with different information. When you contact an estate agent in Spain requesting information about a specific property, they proceed to list you as their client to protect their future business with you. Whether or not you ever actually meet up with this agent or even have any further contact with them, you will remain as their client in certain property databases.

Why can this be a Problem?

In some situations, agents have been known to refuse property viewings on shared properties as a client appears to have registered with many agents which would result in sales commissions being split several ways. As a purchaser you may not be aware of this but as an agent it can be extremely frustrating. All in all, it means that you are not receiving the best service.

How can you Disentangle this Maze?

By registering with professional property finding service such as www.Spanish-Property.net, you ensure that you are assigned to a suitable agent that will look after all your property search requirements. As your representative, they will ensure that you receive the highest quality service before, during and after the property purchase process.

What Should You Look For in an Estate Agent in Spain?

• Experience: Ask for testimonials and what previous experience they have.

• Coverage: Do they have the coverage required and the partnerships in place on the ground to cover your requirements? It is a collaborative business and going the extra mile and also location will make a big difference.

• Knowledge of the Market: Ask the difficult questions about every aspect of living in Spain. If they cannot, or will not, answer them then consider looking for another agent to work with.

• Language ability: How can you expect somebody who cannot communicate in Spanish to know about any problems and encumbrances that may be on the property?

• Employ an English speaking bi-lingual estate agent to represent you as they will notice any problems during the purchasing process.

• Don't fall for the hype. High pressure sales techniques are usually because of pressure to sell and a commission basis to wages. Remember you are paying a lot of money for this purchase and you should get it right first time.

Some Tricks to be Aware of

• If you are first taken to view unsuitable properties, out of your price range, not fulfilling minimum requirements etc. do not be surprised. Spanish and foreign estate agents have long used this tactic to soften you up for the house they really want to sell you which will be the last one in the day. Prepare the shortlists for viewing with your chosen property finder before you go.

• Try not to believe the "Another couple have just looked and are going to put a deposit down tomorrow" line. Sometimes it may be true, but 90% of the time it isn't.

• Have a deposit ready so that you can secure a property at short notice. Money still talks and some sellers will accept an offer lower than the asking price when a deposit is on the table. Do remember that provided the deposit is lodged with a lawyer, it is not at risk. Should there be any problems with the property, your deposit will be returned to you.

• Don't worry about sleeping on it. Usually the property will still be available the next day, despite what the agent says. An early phone call the following day and quick payment of a small deposit will secure the place. But do work with your agent and communicate clearly.

• If the house is newly painted have a really good look for cracks or water damage. You know why. The Spanish do not usually present a house for sale and therefore if it is freshly painted then often the worst sins are possibly hidden. At least wallpaper hiding huge cracks is not a problem here.

• Go to the house again, either on your own or at another time of day to make sure you see it not just when the agent wants you there. A nearby working quarry or traffic jams outside your door may change your mind about a place. Equally it might make you more determined to get it as you can see it in the evening and notice the spectacular sunsets on the terrace and how quiet and peaceful everything is.

Buying "Direct from the Owner" might not be all it seems

There is nothing inherently different about a private sale compared with the purchase of a house through an agent. However the words "caveat emptor" ("let the buyer beware") were never more apt.

When you go looking around any area in Spain you will see lots of "Se Vende" signs on the front of houses and balconies.

This, of course, means "For Sale".

Many of them are not really private sales; they are agents trying to look as if they are private individuals.

Why? Because a lot of Spanish people do not like agents.

However, on private sales you must be careful and it cannot be over emphasised the importance of getting a lawyer or professional advice because many people try to sell without using an agent to avoid the costs but also to avoid the problems that they know accompany the house in the hope of hiding them.

If the conveyancing process is not followed then you may not find out about the dual carriageway that will be ploughing through your garden next year or the compulsory purchase order so that your land is now the 17th fairway of the proposed new golf course with a ridiculously low compulsory purchase price to be given to you.

There are problems associated with buying in Spain at times; it is not always an easy process.

Good professional advice is essential.

After all an outlay of a couple of thousand Euros now, can save you possibly hundreds of thousands in the future.

Do I need the Services of a Lawyer?

Our answer to this question, as an agency, has always been "every time". However, it must be said that if you are getting a mortgage it is less necessary because the bank will make sure that there are no problems on the property as they don't want a worthless asset on their hands if they need to repossess. Any bank supplying a mortgage will do the conveyancing in the background for their own purposes. They will not tell you anything about it but be sure that it will be done.

A good lawyer that you choose should do the following:

• Check out the property registry

• Check the local council records for debts on the property and plans

• Check out the catastro for plans

• Cross check the above with the actual size of the house to look for extensions etc. that have not been declared.

• Check for wills and others who may be contesting the right to sell the property.

• Obviously check that the person selling the house is the owner and has the right to do so.

• Act as a confidante and somebody that you can place your trust in on your major purchase in Spain. If they do not offer the above services, cannot speak your language and do not have good references then think again about using them.

Many people say you should not accept the lawyer proposed by the sellers' agent, as they have a common interest in deceiving you. Sometimes this is true, so here it is useful to decide whether you are confident or not.

Many of the bigger agents and developers have lawyers that work exclusively for them so the conflict of interests is evident. We have always recommended lawyers but do not mind working with others who have already been chosen by the client.

The working relationship between the lawyer and agent is very important to make the process go smoothly and remember that the agent may well know who the bad lawyers are so have a good think about whether to use the recommended lawyer or not.

Should I give my Lawyer Power of Attorney?

Most lawyers, once given power of attorney, will efficiently carry out all necessary bureaucratic and legal procedures related to your property purchase, including NIE applications, dealing with utility companies etc.

This is in addition to the required legal property checks mentioned previously. This can save you a lot of time and headaches.

A power of attorney is usually signing over all of your possessions in Spain so it is a very far reaching document.

It is often open ended too so it is best to take a couple of precautions.

Firstly, once the lawyer has done what he needs to do then take back their copy of the powers.

Only original documents are accepted by notaries and therefore nothing can be done without your say so if you hold the original documents. However you should not revoke the powers as they may be useful in the future and what is the point of doing them again.

Once you have a power of attorney then keep it but you hold the document.

Powers of attorney can also be limited to acting on your behalf on a single issue.

However these are very limited in scope and often present problems because they have been signed to buy a particular property with a reference number, catastral reference and address but if one detail is wrong on the documents, which quite often happens, then they are useless.

The wider the scope of the powers the more useful they are long term.

By taking basic precautions they cannot be abused.

Time to take a look at Shortlisted Properties: The Inspection Visit.

There are usually two types of visit. The guided tour and the self-planned visit where you arrange visits with agents in the local area.

The Guided Tour will usually make sure that you buy off plan and will not show you anything second hand that might interest you. They will not listen to you and make sure that high pressure techniques are used to get you into buying. Why? Off plan properties are generally paid to the agent at high commission rates. Second hand properties are not really as well paid. However hard you try, you will not be able to get these properties at lower prices because the builder and developer are tied into contracts with the agents promoting the properties.

The Self-Planned Visit is the one that we help organise with you. Make sure to get in touch with the agent a couple of days/weeks/months before you come over having built your shortlist online with them with your requirements. This is the armchair option. The more honest you are with the agent about your requirements; price, type of property, size, area etc., the better the chance that a good agent will be able to find you what you want. Get in touch a couple of weeks before to touch base and make the agent aware of what you want exactly.

When you find a place that you really want then it is imperative that you have a deposit ready to put down.

If you return to the UK then do a transfer to the agent, invariably you will find that Murphy's Law works perfectly and somebody else has put the deposit down before you. Obviously we have stated before that the property is more than likely to be still available the next day so don't put a deposit down in haste.

However, if you let too much time pass, have set your heart on a place and really want it you can virtually guarantee that somebody else will beat you to the deposit.

Yes, this is the case even in the buyer's market we are in at the moment, people buy every day in Spain and the Islands so do not be complacent.

I Have Found a Property I Want to Buy. So, What Happens Now?

Once you have found a property you want to buy, the first step is to put in a verbal offer. If you are offering below the asking price, it is advisable to let your agent know how flexible your offer is as they can negotiate on your behalf. Remember, making a silly offer that is too low may jeopardise further negotiations.

Once your offer has been verbally accepted, it is advisable to appoint a lawyer.

However, should you wish to make initial enquiries yourself, we recommend the following:

• Obtain a copy of the Nota Simple form the Property Registry Office. This document identifies the owner of the property and provides details of any outstanding mortgage or embargoes on the property.

• Request receipts for IBI (impuestos sobre bienes inmuebles) payments which will show the valor catastral of the property. Your local taxes and annual property income tax are calculated on this rate.

• If the property is in an urbanisation or part of a community, ask the administrator or president for copies of charges paid.

• If the property is a new build, obtain a copy of the "declaración de obra nueva" and, if applicable "declaración de alteración de bienes naturaleza urbana".

In order for the property to be taken off the market, you will be required to pay a small holding deposit (this amount is negotiable between agents). At this point, your lawyer will prepare a formal offer and agreement contract.

Once the lawyer has conducted all the relevant searches on the property, usually around 2 weeks after the holding deposit has been paid, the exchange of private contracts (contrato privado) takes place.

The private contract sets out terms and conditions of the sale, including the agreed price and a completion date. It is normal practice to pay 10% of the selling price at the time of signing this contract.

Once this contract has been signed, by law, if the purchaser withdraws, any deposit paid is lost. It is also not unusual for clauses to be added to the private contract that should the seller withdraw, then twice the paid deposit should be paid to the purchaser. Ensure your legal representative explains these clauses to you.

On the assigned day, the purchaser and seller (and/or their authorised representatives) are required to be present at the Notary office to sign the title deeds (escritura de compraventa) and if a mortgage is required, the bank manager will be present to also sign the mortgage deeds (escritura de hipoteca).

The role of the notary is not to check the content of the deeds, but merely to confirm that all parties have agreed to them. For this reason, it is advisable to request a copy of the deeds before going to the notary and have them translated and explained to you. One important factor is that the deeds must state that the property is sold "free of charges, mortgages and tenants" (libre de cargas).

Upon signing the deeds, the balance of payment is made and the purchaser takes possession of the property and is the new owner of a property in Spain.

NOTE: This is merely an introduction to buying property in Spain. This subject is a full book in itself. My aim is just to make you start to think about what you should be looking at and the questions you should be asking when you are at the stage of considering buying a property in Spain. If this is what you are thinking about and would like further advice, do not hesitate to contact me.

A great source of information is a book by Nick Snelling, "How to Buy Property and Move to Spain Safely", you can get an updated Kindle / Ebook here: http://movesafelytospain.com/

Buying Property: Our Story

Part One

Finally, it looks like we have a buyer for our house in France. They have paid the deposit, signed the pre sales contact (compromis de vente) and are measuring up for the work they plan to carry out. So, fingers crossed … it is looking good! But please do not ask me how much money we have lost.

So, once again, we are in search of a new home.

Having considered the option of continuing with a long term rental, we have decided that we want to buy a house in Spain. Despite the fact that there are very negative changes, for us, in the mortgage tax relief criteria "desgravación fiscal vivienda" that will come into place in 2011 and our situation with Capital Gains Tax (plusvalía) to be paid if we do not reinvest in Spain before the end of the year, we are determined to do our research and not rush, nor be pushed, into anything that is not 100% what we want.

As we had lived in the Mijas area for the past eighteen months and having spent a lot of time looking at all other areas along the Costa del Sol, we have decided that this is where we want to be for now. I am not going to be unrealistic and say "forever" … I am a realist, after all!

We have carried out searches all over the internet, we check in all local publications, newspapers, free magazines, property brochures, in both Spanish and English and so have a pretty good idea of what we would like and how much we can "hope" to get it for.

As it is such a time consuming task, we also enlisted the help of some local estate agents. This last decision however, proved to be not so much of a time consuming, but a time wasting measure… this comment is not directed at all estate agents, but please can you tell me *"how you expect to sell me a house when you do NOT listen to neither my requests nor past experiences?"*

"Do you really think that telling me that 'Entrerios', which is an inland, relatively under developed rural area, approximately half an hour from the coast , is the new 'Sotogrande', which is a luxury harbour area, is really going to make me buy this house?" … Oh, please!

To further rub salt into the wound, despite being told about our current situation, having made a big mistake buying a house in France, he kept telling us how he loved France and how much this area reminded him of France … get me out of here!

Needless to say, our search continued, with other agents, and we soon found something rather exciting.

Part Two

As we said in Part one, we were considering buying a house in Spain and trying not to rush into things. However, there are many factors that were influencing our decisions. One of those is the fact that 2010 marked the end of automatic entitlement to tax relief on property purchases, (la desgravacion fiscal por compra de vivienda), in Spain.

From January 1st 2011, anyone with a declared annual income (renta annual) in excess of twenty-four thousand euros, no longer qualified for automatic mortgage tax relief.

In a nutshell, this basically meant that:

• Anyone with a declared annul income over 24,107€, that purchased a property in Spain after 31.12.10 was no longer be entitled to the tax relief previously offered in relation to the interest on mortgage payments.

• Anyone who purchased a property in Spain, with a declared annual income equal or inferior to 17,724€ will be entitled to a total deduction of tax relief and in the following year, a total of 15% up to the amount 9,040€

• Anyone with a declared annual income between these two amounts, 17,724€ and 24,107€, continued to enjoy mortgage tax relief calculated in a regressive manner. i.e. a calculated percentage of relief that diminishes once we reach a salary of 24,107€

Confused yet? Even having read this many times I still was ...

So, if we consider that the current mortgage tax relief assumes an annual rebate of up to 1,350€ based on 15%, capped at 9,015€. This would mean that over a 40 year mortgage we would receive a tax rebate of over 50,000€. Now, that is a lot of money to miss out on!

Some autonomous regions, such as Navarra, were continuing to offer the rebate but could we rely on this happening?

Property experts continue to disagree on the immediate future of the Spanish property market. Will prices continue to fall or will they even out? The only fact they seem to agree on is that prices are unlikely to reach previous highs and are not likely to increase in the immediate future.

Mortgages were obviously much more affordable at that moment due to the fact that the Euribor was at around 1.5% compared to 5.38% in September 2008. However, what would happen in the coming months? Who knows and how much risk were we willing to take? What might seem like an amazing deal today may become a noose around our neck in the future …

Anyway, we sent an email to the estate agent to ask his advice on our proposed offer before we actually made it.

Part Three

...And so the house hunting in Spain saga continued .... At the end of the last part, the ongoing story of our attempt at buying property in Spain, and explaining the changes in mortgage tax relief that were due to come into effect, from January 2011 in Spain, we had sent an email to the estate agent to ask his advice on our proposed offer on a house that we had seen and very much liked. The news was not good. He said that the sellers would not accept such a low offer and advised us of a minimum price that he believed he could negotiate for us.

And so the game began ... How do you know if the estate agent is playing games? How do we really know that the sellers would refuse a low offer? Did he make the offer or was he simply trying to get a better price from us? On one hand, you want to secure the best price possible within your budget. On the other hand, I do also believe that you can lose a good property if you barter too much over the price.

After a few days of deliberation and many more property viewings, we decided to put in an offer which was higher than the original suggestion but still below the "advised" minimum offer price. We decided that if the offer was accepted then we would go ahead and if it was rejected then we would continue with our long term rental and keep looking. The pressure would be off, as we would have missed the final date for the tax relief.

One phone call later and a slight increase on our behalf, after a final push by the agent, (still below the minimum I must add!) and the offer was put forward. Within twenty-four hours, the offer was accepted and it was full steam ahead.

Now the race against time was on. Next, was going to the bank to talk about mortgages in Spain.

Part Four

House hunting … the Never Ending Story: The clock was ticking, the days and weeks were passing by and we were still waiting to sign the sales contract to buy our new house in Spain. Yes, the same house we decided to buy back in November.

The good news was that, thanks to the fiscal advice provided by our associates at CCB Spain, we still qualified for the mortgage tax relief as we had signed the Private Sales Contract and paid our 10% deposit in December 2010, before the law in Spain changed.

However, the fact that the sale of the house was an inheritance case and to complicate issues further, one of the beneficiaries was a minor had seriously slowed the process down. A fact that was not disclosed by the estate agent until our offered price was accepted and we had made our decision that this was the house we wanted.

Many of you may be wondering why we still waited … in the end it was worth it, I can tell you!

In the meantime, we had been speaking to Spanish banks to get a mortgage and of course, getting the best mortgage with a bank in Spain is not so easy at the moment. We have also been looking into the different types of insurance in Spain, some of which are obligatory when applying for a mortgage with Spanish banks.

Mortgages and Insurance in Spain is another story…

Money Matters

"It is a good idea to set up a non-resident bank account in Spain, during the early stages of planning your move."

Preparation

Taking a bit of time to sort your finances before moving to Spain, can save you a considerable amount of money and also stress. Here are a few starting points ...

Speak to professionals for financial advice

Contact a financial advisor, ideally one who has specific experience in Spain.

This person can advise you on pensions, tax liabilities and what is necessary to do in terms of fiscal responsibilities in Spain.

Questions that you should be asking at this point include: if you are keeping a residence in the UK and planning to rent it out how is the income taxed?

If you work part of the year in the UK how will that affect fiscal residency?

These can all be answered on a case-by-case basis by an experienced Financial Advisor.

Inform the HMRC (Hmrc.gov.uk) – there are certain forms that must be filled in including form P85 – Leaving the UK.

Money Transfer Companies and Bank Accounts

Firstly, your British bank accounts. Ensure you have internet banking set up before you leave the country; also make sure that all your statements are being sent electronically and your debit and credit cards are up-to-date.

Check transfer costs with your existing UK bank and have a look at what different UK banks offer. Keep an eye out for things like free European transfers. If you are going to be transferring funds from the UK to Spain, no matter how big or small, it is worth setting up with an account with a currency transfer company. Many people lose money by using their UK bank cards to withdraw cash when abroad. A little forward thinking can save you money.

Contact me at info@ccbspain.com for a referral to a reputable money exchange company.

Once you have an IBAN for a Spanish bank account, transferring funds is a simple matter.

Understanding your Spanish Bank Account Number

Spanish bank account numbers are made up of 20 digits. For example: 2100 2527 33 1234567890

- 2100 is the name of the bank (ie. La Caixa)
- 2527 is the branch code (ie. Mijas Pueblo)
- 33 is the security code
- 1234567890 is the 10 digit account number.

Whenever you are asked for your bank account details in Spain, you should provide the full 20 digits.

Other bank codes you will be given that are necessary for international money transfers are:

IBAN: International Bank Account Number

BIC/Codigo Swift: Bank Identifier Code / The Society for Worldwide Interbank Financial Telecomunications

The IBAN is made up of a maximum of 34 characters:

Eg: ES21 2100 2527 33 123456789
- ES = the country code
- 21 = security control code
- Plus 20 digits of the full account number.

The BIC/Codigo Swift is made up a 8 – 11 characters:
Eg. CAIXESMAXXX
- CAIX = Name of bank
- ES = Country of origin
- MA = Location of the banks central office (town or region)
- XXX = Location of a specific office or department of the bank

Whenever possible, it is a good idea to set up a non-resident bank account in Spain, during the early stages of planning your move.

Opening a non-resident account is a simple process that requires only your passport as ID.

You will sign a statement confirming that you are a tax resident in your home country.

Once you become residents in Spain, your account can be changed. Having a non-resident account means that your annual costs will be higher than those of a resident.

This is usually only a minimal amount and the convenience compensates for the price difference.

Most banks will immediately issue you with a bank book (una

libreta) that you can use to withdraw funds and a debit/visa card is issue within about 5 days.

Many Spanish banks offer online banking in English and so you can manage your accounts from wherever you are.

Having an account open means that you can start to send funds to Spain and have the use of debit / credit cards as soon as you arrive. This is particularly useful for having deposits for rental properties, signing telephone and internet contracts and of course, applying for residency.

Taking your Pets to Spain

For some families, organising the transportation of family pets to Spain can be as stressful as making arrangements for the rest of the family. Once again, forethought and preparation can massively reduce these stress levels. In general, there are two decisions to be made when transporting pets: the self-drive method or using a pet transport company. Whichever of these two methods you decide is best for you, the following information is essential reading.

An Essential Checklist for a safe journey with pets

- Has your pet been micro chipped and is the microchip number correctly inserted in the passport?
- Was your pet vaccinated with rabies after the microchip was inserted?
- Has the vet validated the entries in the passport?
- Does your pet have water, absorbent bedding and adequate ventilation for the journey?
- Do you have sufficient poo bags?
- If your pet has a long journey ahead give your pet a light meal before it goes at least two hours before the journey and remember to pack small snacks for them
- Pets are susceptible to diet change so take adequate supplies of their normal food.
- Do not forget your pet bowls
- Be aware there are more biting insects abroad than in the UK. Ask your vet how you can take a preventative steps for your pets in advance (**please read hazards for pets in Spain p.129)

- Purchase a great little tool for removing ticks " The tick hook" is an essential tool to have in your pet's first aid box
- Ensure that your pet travels with a secure collar & lead with a suitable ID Tag with your contact details on
- Ensure your pet is clean, bathed & groomed prior to the journey to make the journey pleasant for the animal & sweet smelling in the vehicle for you!!

Questions to Ask and Points to Consider

Here are some questions to ask and points to look out for if choosing a Pet Transport Company to transport your pets.

Travel By Land

The first question you should ask is if the Pet Transporter is licensed to transport animals. In our opinion this should be the *minimum* requirement you should be looking for and ask for proof that this is the case.

All licensed transporters will have a plaque on their vehicle and some companies will have a copy of their license displayed on their website there should also be up to date photos of their current vehicles internally as well as externally.

In complying to be licensed, the vehicle will have been inspected and approved by DEFRA (Department for Environment, Food and Rural Affairs) to ensure that there is adequate ventilation as well as a list of other factors including clean, safe compartments for your pets to travel in.

Most pet transporters will have a clear, professional and concise website for you to look at and you should be able to submit a request for a quotation.

In their response to you, you should feel that your pet is going to travel with the best care possible.

They should be able to give you clear information on the journey, how your pet will travel, the route, overnight stops and timings as well as provide updates during the journey preferably with photographs of your (dogs) **being walked**.

You should be made to feel comfortable with whom you choose. We would recommend that you send off at least 3 pet transport enquiry forms to various companies.

The journey to Spain from the UK is quite long and if you are not used to long journeys in a vehicle it is always sensible to put the care of your pet in the hands of a professional animal transporter as they are used to such journeys and they will know the nicest stops in order to exercise your pet's safely.

You must ask the right questions and this type of service will more than likely be a "door to door" service but remember do not always go for the cheapest quotes as cheaper is not always better.

Travel by Plane

This is probably the quickest way to transport your pets but it has its downside too. You can go direct to the airlines in the first instance and they will point you in the right direction to an airline agent to help you transport your animals.

You will have to organise your own Pet Travel Crates which will have to be IATA airline approved and there are strict guidelines on the measurements of your pet in conjunction with your crate but the agent will guide you.

Usually travel by plane is the more expensive option and you will have to get your pets to the airports yourself.

All pets travelling in & out of the UK have to travel as cargo with the luggage and sometimes this can be quite traumatic for your pet as well you the owner.

You just need to choose the right method of travel for you and your pet.

Documentation Requirements EU Pet Passports

From 1ˢᵗ January 2012, all pet dogs, cats and ferrets can enter or re-enter the UK from any country in the world without quarantine, provided they meet the rules of the Pet Travel Scheme.

Make sure you have had the procedures carried out in the correct order and your pet's documentation is correctly completed. If you do not, your pet may not be able to enter the country or may have to be licensed into quarantine on arrival. This will mean delay and will cost you money.

Here are some important details about the Pet Travel Scheme to comply with the rules of travelling with Dogs, cats & ferrets into France & Spain:

All pets must have a valid **DEFRA approved** passport showing that your pet has been micro-chipped so it can be properly identified and vaccinated with rabies. The order of preparation is critical:

- The Microchip must be implanted before the rabies vaccination or on the same day.
- The valid **DEFRA approved** pet passport must show that the rabies vaccination entry has been correctly completed with the full Manufacturer & Vaccine product name and validated with the official veterinarian signature, veterinary stamp and dated.
- 21 days after the rabies vaccination your pet can cross the border into France and Spain

Remember, your pet can be stopped from travelling if the details in their record are in the wrong place.

Re-register Your Pet's Microchip on Arrival

It is so important for your pet's safety to ensure that when you move home, particularly to another country, that you re-register your pet's microchip to your new address.

This will save any upset if your dog should become lost in the first few days of arriving at your new home.

A pet tag is also far quicker means of identification than a microchip.

You, the owner, can be contacted immediately avoiding a stressful search for your beloved pet or the potential waiting that comes with microchip identification.

It is also easier for the person who has found the pet to contact the first available number on an identification tag.

Many animals end up at animal shelters because they simply have no means of identification, this can be traumatic for both the pet & owner.

Why not increase the chance of being re-united with your pet by ordering an ID tag before setting off on your journey.

In many European Countries now it is law that a dog should have a microchip but also display an ID tag with the owner's address / location details on it.

To re-register your microchip in Spain you simply have to go to your new veterinary hospital and re-register your pet with them and the vets will sort the paperwork.

This costs around €12.00. At present, you can only do this at the vets in Spain as there is no facility to do this on-line.

If, however, you are returning to the UK, you can re-register your details on-line please visit: www.pettrac.co.uk

Returning to the UK

If you are contemplating **returning Pets to the UK** and your Dog, Cat or Ferret's Passport is up to date, (*the rabies vaccination is in date*) then you should have no problem with transporting your Pets to the UK.

Make certain that your Pet's Passport has no alterations or crossed out entries, in which case these entries must be stamped & signed by the Veterinarian.

It must be noted that a Pet Passport must have **"no correction fluid"** to alter mistakes. It will not be accepted at the UK border. No alterations are allowed to be made without initial & stamp and the passport to be completed in ink only.

Tapeworm treatment – (dogs only): **before** entering the UK, all pet dogs (including assistance dogs) must be treated for tapeworm. The treatment must be administered by an official veterinarian not less than 24 hours and not more than 120 hours (1-5 days) before its scheduled arrival time in the UK.

There is no mandatory requirement for tick treatment or blood tests anymore if traveling in from an EU country.

It is the sole responsibility of the owner/escort to ensure that they have the correct documentation for bringing an animal in or out of the UK.

It is essential that you check this.

The owner is the only person responsible for any errors in the pet passport.

Incorrectly completed and dated documents may result in your pet being refused travel & quarantined at your expense.

You should give particular attention to the timing of the microchip implantation, rabies vaccination & tapeworm treatment.

Dangerous Dog License

Update from May 2012 Dangerous Dogs

The Junta de Andalucia has added Bull terriers, Presa Canarios, Napolitan mastiffs and Boxers to the list.

These breeds cannot be taken out in public without a lead and muzzle and must be registered at the town hall.

Dangerous Dogs

Any person owning a potentially dangerous dog (perros potencialmente peligrosos) in Spain must have an appropriate license (by law of article 3 of the Royal Decree 287/2002, of 22 of March 2002) and the dog must be registered with the municipality.

Handlers and walkers of dangerous or potentially dangerous dogs must also be licensed (article 1, 2 of Law 50/1999, of December 1999).

A license is valid for five years.

Potentially dangerous dogs are identified as being in one of three categories:

1) Breeds and breed crosses classified as potentially dangerous:
- Doberman (Andalucia only)
- Bull Terriers
- Presa Canarios
- Napolitan Mastiffs
- Boxers
- Pit Bull Terrier
- Staffordshire Bull Terrier
- American Staffordshire Terrier

- Rottweiler
- Dogo Argentino
- Fila Brasileiro
- Tosa Inu
- Akita Inu

2) Dogs with certain characteristics of these breeds are also classified as potentially dangerous. The characteristics are:

- Strong musculature, powerful or athletic constitution, robustness, agility, vigour and endurance
- Short hair
- Deep chest (60 to 80 cm), height of over 50 cm and a weight over 20 Kg
- Big, square, head, with a wide skull and strong jaws
- Broad, short and muscled neck.
- Straight, parallel forelegs and muscular hindquarters, relatively long back legs standing at an angle

3) Dogs that have a track record of aggression to humans and other animals must also be licensed and registered.

Dog Owner License Application

The license application is made to the municipality of the place of residence. The applicant must take the following (an applicant must be over 18 years):

- Proof of identity (passport or residence card)
- Proof of having no criminal convictions
- Proof of being mentally and physically capable of looking after one of these animals. (There are centres test of physical and psychological aptitude can be done and a certificate issued. The certificate must have been issued in the previous 12 months)
- An insurance contract for the dog with a liability of at least €120,000 (€175,000 in Andalucia)

- Proof of fully up-to-date vaccinations
- Proof of identification by microchip
- Proof that the dog is or has attended training school

Once accepted, a license (the licencia para tener perros potencialmente peligrosos) is issued.

Dog Registration

Potentially dangerous dogs must be registered with the municipal registry for dangerous dogs (Registro Municipal de Perros Potencialmente Peligrosos). The registration of the dog must be renewed annually.

The documents you require to register the dog are:
- Proof of identification and microchip number's certificate
- Certificate from the vet stating that the dog is in good health

Walking a Potentially Dangerous Dog

Dog owners or handlers must carry the licence and dog registration document when out with the dog.

The dog must be muzzled and on a lead of no more than two metres long (one metre in Andalucia).

Only one dog may be handled per person.

In Andalucia, dangerous animals are banned from entering children's leisure or recreational areas.

Note: In most municipalities, only one dog may be registered to one person. The property where the dogs are kept must be enclosed by a two metre high barrier.

So, you've read some essential information about preparing your pet for their journey to Spain and the paperwork you need to get organised.

Now we need to consider the risks your pet may face in Spain.

If you are bringing your pet to Spain, it is advisable to read about the possible risks the animals may face.

The following information is not intended to scare you.

It is merely to provide you with important information in case you come across these hazards.

I believe that by having this information in advance, you are more likely to be able to avoid incidents or, at least, know how to react when an incident occurs.

Hazards for Pets in Spain

Biting Insects, crawling critters these are essential things that you need to know about for you and your pet's welfare

Leishmaniasis is a Serious Disease

This disease mainly affects dogs, although occasionally cases have been reported in human and other animals, such as cats.

It's caused by a parasite and transmitted by insects similar to mosquitoes (sand flies), as known as "The mosquito's disease".

When a sand fly bites an infected dog, it acquires the illness and after a short latency period, it transmits the disease to all the animals that it bites, thus expanding the disease.

It's important to know: ***Both, parasites and mosquitoes are present in Spain, especially in the South, because of the weather.***

In the Autonomous Community of Andalucía, all Leishmania's cases must be declared to the competent authorities, and those animals who are not treated are supposed to be put down.

Leishmaniasis is a serious pathology, with multiple symptoms and often lethal.

Between the symptoms can be found: depression, lethargy, anorexia, skin lesions (ulcers, crusts, inflammation and secondary infections), nasal bleeding, kidney and hepatic problems, anaemia, etc.

Not all breeds are equally susceptible.

Vaccine Information

(The New Vaccine is now available in Spain)

Why should you vaccinate?

The appearance of symptoms depends on the kind of immunity response that the animal develops:

One of the clinical signs is because it generates too many antibodies that cause damage in different organs. This is the one that animals develop in normal situation. The other one favours the parasite's elimination and disease resistance.

Furthermore, it produces memory cells which keep the animal protected from future infections.

This kind of response is stimulated by the vaccine.

This vaccine is safe, since for its elaboration they have used a culture media free of protein (the main cause of allergic reactions).

Likewise, the residual virulence has been reduced (minor side effects, such as: fever, depression, anorexia, etc) as they don't use the full parasite, just microscopic parts of it.

Immunisation

Worm 10 days before vaccination; in case the animal is infested, otherwise the vaccine will lose part of its efficacy.

Vets must do a quick blood test to determinate if the animal is infected, because sometimes there aren't any symptoms until later on.

If the animal is positive the vaccine is useless.

Primary vaccination: 3 doses, 21 days apart between them, followed by an annual booster.

Leishmaniasis Summary

1. Leishmaniasis is a serious illness, so that we must fight against it with all the tools of vet's disposal. This includes: vaccination, the use of sand fly's repellents (collar or drops). Recommendations are the use of the Scalibor collar & or Advantix spot on drops or the new Vectra 3D Spot on. Avoid if possible keeping your pet outdoors at dawn and dusk.

2. Thanks to the vaccination it avoids the need of symptomatic treatment, warranting pet's health and reducing costs in medication and analytical checks.

3. The vaccination not only protects animals from the infection, but also reduces the number of infected animals and therefore the dissemination of the illness to other animals or places

The Processionary Caterpillar

At the end of the winter when the weather is beginning to warm up, it is the time to warn pet owners of the dangers of the "candy floss" white nests that appear rapidly in the fir trees above our heads!!

This is the nest of the PROCESSIONARY CATERPILLAR and they arrive in their thousands!! – They are dangerous to humans too but because dogs & cats are inquisitive & like to nosey about on the ground sniffing out what's new – that is when pets get themselves into trouble.

The caterpillars get their name because they follow each other in a "procession" actually looking quite sweet, innocent and cute; they are dark brown in colour with white hair.

The caterpillars hatch from their nests and follow each other across a pathway or road making a definite line to their onward destination.

It is at this point that we canines and felines wander up to the "little monsters" & have a good sniff to investigate the findings – & get into trouble.

If your pet comes into contact with the caterpillars it is imperative that you thoroughly wash the contact area AND get your pet to a veterinarian **as soon as possible.**

The caterpillars are covered in thousands of tiny hairs which get hooked on the skin, mouth or nose – they will embed into pets and then literally "eat the flesh away".

The Caterpillars are attracted to Pine Trees. **Avoid exercising pets in the pine forests until the end of April.**

The Poison Toad

If you notice your dog foaming at the mouth after messing with a toad, immediately rinse it out with water.

If the dog eats the toad, you should get it to a vet or animal hospital right away.

Here in Spain the giant toad can grow up to eight inches long and is very heavy. This toad is greenish-brown and covered with bumps. It has glands that can secrete a very toxic poison. The Giant toad is responsible for the death of many dogs. This toad will come into gardens and eat the dogs' food. If the dog grabs the toad it will be poisoned, immediately.

Pet owners might notice these signs: frothy salivation with vigorous head shaking, pawing at the mouth and continuous efforts to vomit, uncoordinated movement and staggering.

If you know of or strongly suspect toad poisoning, immediately rinse out your pet's mouth with water before going to your veterinarian or an emergency clinic for treatment. Most toad poisonings occur in the evening or the night.

Unfortunately, there are no antidotes for toad venom intoxication, but many of these victims may be saved with symptomatic treatment, which reduces the absorption of toxin and controls the clinical signs of illness.

Depending upon circumstances, your veterinarian may use a variety of drugs to control heart abnormalities, breathing problems and excitation of the central nervous system.

The key to survival is rapid recognition of signs and prompt veterinary medical care

Tick Fever & Lymes Disease

Ticks are fairly common ectoparasites of dogs and cats. How often you see ticks on your dog and how severe a tick assault will be depends on the region of the country in which you live but you will definitely be in contact with them if you are moving to Spain; the time of year (tick activity varies in warm and cool weather), the habits of your dog particularly, and how and when you use tick control products. Some ticks can infest dogs that spend most of their time indoors, and even dogs that only spend brief periods of time outside can have ticks.

How will Ticks Affect my Pet?

Ticks attach to your dog by inserting their mouthparts into your dog's skin. Many ticks also produce a sticky, glue like substance that helps them to remain attached.

After attaching to your dog, ticks begin feeding on your dog's blood.

The places where ticks attach can become red and irritated.

Although rare, ticks can consume enough of your dog's blood to cause a deficiency called anaemia.

Certain female ticks can also cause a rare paralysis in dogs as a result of a toxin they produce while feeding.

More important, ticks are capable of causing many diseases in your pet.

The disease with which most people are familiar is called Lyme disease.

Lyme disease can cause arthritis and swelling of your dog's joints, resulting in painful lameness.

Rocky Mountain spotted fever can cause fever, lameness, and other signs.

There are also other diseases that ticks can transmit to your dog. Your veterinarian can answer questions about the diseases that are important where you live.

How do I Prevent my Pets from Getting Ticks?

It is very difficult to prevent your dog's exposure to ticks. Ticks can attach to your dog or cat when he or she goes with you on walks, hikes, or during any outdoor activities.

The best way to prevent ticks from attaching to your dog is by the regular use of tick control products. Your veterinarian can advise you about the best product for your dog and your situation. Your veterinarian is also aware of diseases that are common in your area and can pose a risk to your dog.

If you have a tick problem in your garden or yard consider:

- Treating the outdoor environment (be sure to understand what products you are using and how they affect the environment)
- Making a landscape change to make the environment less tick friendly – this can be done by providing a 3 foot buffer between the lawn and any woods. Mulch, wood chips, or gravel work well, and help to decrease the migration of ticks into yards, ridding your yard of wild animals will help too.

Often more ticks are present or they are more active at certain times of the year.

Are Ticks Dangerous to Humans?

Ticks can attach to and feed on humans. The skin where ticks attach to humans can become red and irritated.

It is important to realize that people do not get these diseases from their dogs.

Both people and dogs get the diseases from ticks they come into contact with outdoors.

Diseases, such as Lyme disease which have already been described in dogs, can also be very serious in humans.

Did you know?

While ticks themselves cause only mild irritation, they can carry diseases that pose a serious threat to animals and humans. Ticks can be prevented by regular use of tick control products.

Just pulling off a tick can leave body parts attached to your dog.

Purchase a tick removal tool. Illnesses transmitted by ticks can cause fever, anaemia, paralysis, lameness, and other symptoms.

People cannot catch Lyme disease from infected dogs, but the same ticks that bite dogs can cause these illnesses and others if they bite humans.

Adult ticks can live up to 3 years without a blood meal.

Ticks live on three different animals during their life.

Most ticks spend most of their life OFF the host (animal) in the environment.

Ticks can't jump and don't "fall from trees" as most people think, but transfer onto hosts when animals or humans walk through long grass, bushes and are often found around goats /sheep and deer.

Ticks are common in the UK as well as in Spain.

Useful Resources

I would like to thank, Rachel from Posh Pets Spain for confirming the information in this chapter and for providing all the information in the Hazards for Pets in Spain section. We have been extremely happy with the service provided by Rachel's company and would happily recommend them to you. Her contact details are below.

Rachel Goutorbe www.poshpetsspain.com
Pet travel: www.poshpetstravel.com
posh@poshpetsspain.com
Tel: 0034 952 597035

Important UK Information Sources

https://www.gov.uk/take-pet-abroad

Website: www.defra.gov.uk/pets

Email: pettravel@ahvla.gsi.gov.uk

Helpline: +44 (0)870 241 1710

Meeting People and Making Friends

Moving to Spain, or any other country, throws up many challenges that we wouldn't necessarily face in our country of origin. (I prefer not to use the word "home country" as I consider Spain to be my home).

One of the most common questions we are asked refers to the issue of meeting people in Spain. People are often asking how we make new friends.

In this section I am going to focus on ways of making friends, before you move to Spain. In my next book *"Living in Spain with Children"*, I will focus on more location based methods.

For those who have read our interview "Twitter helped us make friends when we moved to Spain" in The Telegraph (see Our Story later in this section), you will know that we believe in the power of social media.

For us, it has been an excellent tool to use for meeting people in Spain. We have had the pleasure of meeting many of our "virtual" friends in the flesh. It is so interesting to meet the real person behind the avatar.

Making friends online takes time.

People are not always who they appear to be.

Be yourself and, if you do it right, you will attract people like yourself.

People you will want to meet in person.

Giving and Sharing

One of the biggest mistakes some people make, when moving to Spain, is changing their natural persona. It's almost like they think, "A new country. A new me!" Now, I'm no psychologist but please, just be yourself! Be happy with who you are and with what you have to give. And do give. Give as much as you can. Give until you think you have nothing more to give. And then give some more.

> *"We make a living by what we get.*
> *We make a life by what we give."*
> **Winston Churchill**

Joining Online Communities

There are online groups and communities in most geographical areas, simply search for them online and tell them what you have to offer.

Facebook is a great tool for getting to know people in a new area before you move to Spain and then you have the opportunity to meet them once you have made the move.

Search the area you are thinking about moving to and you are sure to find several options.

Some are open groups and some you will need to request to join. Take your time to work out which are the better groups.

From these online groups, local meet ups are often organised.

This is particularly true for "Mums & Tots" style groups. It can be very reassuring to develop a relationship with local parents in your chosen area before you even make your move.

It is also a great way of researching the family friendly facilities and activities available to you and, of course, receive first hand feedback about schools and education in the area.

Most local areas have communities where expat residents share hints, tips and real life experiences. Generally, people are willing to share their knowledge in these groups. However, watch out for the grumpy trolls.

From experience, almost every forum style environment has at least one, if not several, grumpy trolls. Grumpy trolls shout the loudest and have an opinion on everything. Their opinions are often negative and detrimental to people's positivity. The trolls believe that because they are unhappy about their life, others do not have the right to give their dreams a chance, They knock you down at every opportunity. They blatantly bad mouth the positive people. I have one piece of advice for you about the trolls … ignore them.

Don't feed the trolls!

Trolls do not want to reason nor hear the truth. They want to spread their misery. If they approach you, online or in person, politely smile and walk away. It will infuriate them.

"Never get tired of doing little things for others, sometimes those little things occupy the biggest parts of their hearts." **Unknown**

Be it in person or be it on social media such as Twitter, Facebook, Linked In, Google+, don't just ask "what's in it for me?". Don't just promote yourself and your business. Share your knowledge. Give people a reason to interact with you.

People love people who give. People love people who share.

Friendships develop from sharing, whether it be sharing knowledge and expertise, sharing ideas or simply sharing your time … never think you have nothing to give nor share.

"You give but little when you give of your possessions. It is when you give of yourself that you truly give." **Kahil Gibran**

When you give and share you need not feel guilty when you then need to ask for help yourself.

I am regularly amazed at the response I receive when I ask for information on social media. There is an abundance of people willing to give and share.

So, what are you waiting for? There are a whole bunch of people waiting to get to know you and to share their knowledge about the area you are hoping to make your new home. Get online and start making friends.

The Next Step

"Keep your feet firmly on the ground. Do your research. Do more research."

A Review of What to Consider before Moving

Here is a quick review of what we have discussed and a few other reminders and extras to bear in mind before you make the big move and what you should do now...

Research the Education Options
Look at the Areas you are considering

Inform yourself of the application procedures and requirements. Ensure your child has a place before looking into property options.

Applications for state schools, as I said earlier, are submitted in March.

Will the school accept your child outside of the usual application periods?

Double check current fees and procedures for private and International schools.

Keep within budget!

Learn the Language

Enrol in a local college while in the UK, to learn the basics.

It takes a long time to be bilingual (and many never even get close), but by starting with a conversational Spanish class at home, you will at least be able to greet people, order food, speak to your children's teachers, and understand basic inferences.

Invest in some textbooks, cd's and even children's dvd's.

Make language learning fun and enjoy it as a family. Consider starting up online Skype classes.

(See the Language chapter for resources and suggestions)

Paperwork

Ensure you have all the necessary documents prepared, as mentioned in our previous chapters.

Check when your passports expire. It is cheaper to renew them whilst you are in your home country rather than via the Embassy in Spain.

When does your driving licence expire? Ensure you have the European licence with the EU symbol and your photograph on it. This is valid for driving in Spain. Once you are a resident in Spain you will not be legally allowed to renew your UK/EU licence. You will be required to swap it for a Spanish licence.

For school registration, ensure you have copies and originals of the full birth certificates of your children. The birth certificates must show the correct names of the parents. These will need to be officially translated for legal purposes. If you need the name of a reliable official translator, please contact me. Medical records showing that the children have received all necessary vaccinations are required.

Remember that once you have moved to Spain, the two most important documents are:

First – your NIE (Numero de Identification de Extranjeros); this is the unique identification number that you and your family need.

The second is being registered as living at your address in that municipality (Empadronamiento), which is similar to the electoral role in the UK.

Your town hall (Ayuntamiento) issues the Empadronamiento certificates and the police station or comisaría issues the NIEs. (See the chapter on NIE & Residency for more details on this matter).

If you would like to have your NIE number before you move, it is possible to give your power of attorney to a lawyer, to make the NIE application on your behalf. However, unless you are purchasing a property, I do not feel this is a necessary expense.

It can easily be sorted on your arrival in Spain.

For more advice and assistance about NIEs and Spanish bureaucracy, visit www.ccbspain.com.

Should I take my Car to Spain?

Save money before you even start your relocation to Spain!

It is worth finding out if it is better to import your current car to Spain or if it is better to buy a car once you get to Spain?

Importing your UK vehicle can be very expensive.

The cost of importing a vehicle to Spain, is based on calculations and prices decided by the official authorities, including:

- A registration tax (or certificate of exemption) – Impuesto de matriculación.
- A road/traffic tax (or certificate of exemption) – impuesto de circulación del ayuntamiento.
- V.A.T. (or certificate of exemption) – IVA.

The calculations are based on make, model, category and age of the vehicle, the weight of the vehicle and carbon emissions.

Be careful of companies who give quotes without having seen your official vehicle documentation.

You must also budget for the special ITV (Spanish MOT) which is currently approximately €130 for cars and €197 for motorbikes. (Please check current prices with your local Spanish MOT centre).

Also, any alterations required to adhere to Spanish traffic laws (usually this entails changing headlights).

With the exception of commercial vehicles, most right hand drive vehicles can be easily imported into Spain without too many complications.

We strongly recommend you obtain two or three quotes before proceeding with importing a UK car to Spain ... you will be amazed by the differing prices companies in Spain charge!

Seriously, please think twice before bringing a RHD vehicle to Spain. It is much easier and safer driving a LHD vehicle here. It may cost you a bit more in the short term but you will be glad you made the decision.

House-Hunting

As I have continually stressed throughout this book, unless you have already spent a considerable amount of time in Spain, I always recommend renting a property before purchasing one.

There is a huge difference between being on holiday somewhere and living there.

Renting for a year to eighteen months prior to buying a property is advisable. A rental contract within your school's catchment area, accompanied by a valid Padrón certificate is as valuable as an escritura (deeds of a house).

No matter how much research you do, it is always possible that one day your situation will change.

You may decide to change school.

You may decide to change area.

You may decide to leave Spain.

Allow yourself time and breathing space to make these decisions.

Rental prices in many parts of Spain are relatively reasonable, so don't feel as though it's a waste of money.

With purchasing fees at between 10 and 12% in Spain, a hasty purchase can easily become a costly mistake.

Without wanting to preach, "that un-missable bargain house" will appear again...

Have a look on websites such as www.kyero.com and www.thinkspain.com for rental options.

If you have the opportunity to use relocation advisors or property finders, like myself, you will have most of the hard work done for you.

Local knowledge is like gold.

Stunning properties on the internet are often not as attractive in real life.

It is easy to hide a busy main road with a camera.

Similarly, it can be difficult to capture the special feel some properties have.

A local relocation agent, who is impartial to estate agencies can be your invaluable eyes and ears on the ground.

Don't forget to contact me for help in the Malaga area or to visit www.spain-property.net for other areas of Spain.

Have a Clear-Out

This may surprise you, but I am often asked about the availability of good furniture, curtain & bedding etc. shops in Spain.

Many people plan to pay expensive shipping fees when moving to Spain as they are uncertain about what they can purchase over here.

In Malaga, we are lucky to have excellent shopping facilities within a short distance of most areas. I am also a huge fan of Amazon who are getting bigger here in Spain too.

As a general rule, unless you are absolutely certain that you have chosen the right area for you and your family to move to, it is often a good idea to leave furniture and bulky belongings in storage at the outset.

It is a lot easier to change rental properties, once in Spain, without the upheaval and added expense of local removal companies, each time you move.

You may be surprised at how many times you do move before you find your ideal home over here!

On the other hand, if you are buying a holiday home or a new home abroad, using a reputable removals company to bring over your personal belongings is an essential part of your relocation process.

If you would like any recommendations, just drop me a line.

Please be advised that we do not work with the cheapest, we work with the best!

Don't waste money on transportation companies for items that may not be necessary.

Don't tempted to bring all your furniture over with you, particularly if you are renting a property.

Besides the cost of delivery, you might find that what looked perfect in an old cottage in an English village doesn't quite work in a Spanish villa or that, with the temperature differences, a formal indoor dining table and chairs would go unused.

Simple items like soft furnishings, small bits of furniture and of course favourite toys are often enough to help children to settle into their new home.

If you require the services of a removal company, contact them now and request quotes.

Removal companies need to plan their trips well in advance.

The more organised you are and the earlier you start looking, the more likely you are to get what you want. (i.e. furniture and belongings that arrive when you need them!)

Don't Burn Your Bridges

Perhaps the best advice above anything else when moving to Spain is: if you can afford to keep a property in the UK (or your country of origin) then do so.

Whether you decide to downsize to a smaller more manageable property or keep your original home.

This gives you options in the future and a possible rental income, too.

For many people, moving to Spain is their dream. They create a little Spanish bubble.

Unfortunately, on too many occasions that bubble bursts and their dream becomes a nightmare. Do not let this happen to you.

Keep your feet firmly on the ground.

Do your research.

Do more research.

Do not be afraid to ask for help in all areas.

A Final Word

So, there you have it. Hopefully, I have given you lots of things to think about, to research and to set you off on the right foot to carefully plan your move to Spain. This book is in no way exhaustive. There are so many things you need to think about and get in order before your move to Spain. If I have raised questions that you had not previously considered then I have accomplished my mission. Remember, I am here if you are still uncertain about making the move. Drop me an email and we'll schedule a phone call. I will never make the decision for you, but I will help you think it through.

You can join us on Facebook:
www.facebook.com/FamilyLifeInSpain

Tweet with us on Twitter:
https://twitter.com/FamilyInSpain

Follow our boards on Pinterest:
http://www.pinterest.com/familyinspain/

Join the community on Google+
https://plus.google.com/u/0/+Familylifeinspain

You can sign up to my websites and keep up to date with new articles and updates.
www.familylifeinspain.com
www.movetomalaga.com
www.movetomijas.com

It is worth typing the following link out and making sure that you watch the free "Moving to Spain with Children" YouTube videos in this playlist: https://www.youtube.com/playlist?list=PLN-cXZkvgEKExX-l3AtVzxpqwEuFnPI4n

You can also subscribe to the YouTube channel. I will be adding more videos regularly.

Don't forget to read Nick Snelling's book "How to Buy Property and Move to Spain Safely", you can get an updated Kindle / EBook here: **http://movesafelytospain.com/**

I also recommend reading *"You and the Law in Spain"* by David Searl. The best-selling complete and readable guide covering every aspect of Spanish laws affecting foreigners. Accurately referred to as "The Bible for foreigners in Spain" by The Times.

Thanks for reading and I look forward to hearing about your successful move to Spain!

Lisa Sadleir

Lisa Sadleir

Lisa Sadleir has lived in Spain since 1991. She now lives in Mijas Pueblo, southern Spain, with her husband and two young children.

Having spent many years answering questions and assisting foreigners moving to and living in Spain, she has a thorough understanding of what people need to know when planning their move to Spain.

You can read her articles on her key websites www.familylifeinspain.com and www.ccbspain.com and she contributes regularly to expat and overseas websites and publications.

My other Books

Having read this book, I hope you have noticed that I am passionate about the importance of learning languages. I have recently designed a series of books for children, to help them learn Spanish. Look out for my language-learning books due to be published soon:

Cooking in our Cocina is an English Spanish Activity Book for children learning Spanish. It is the first in our Cooking with Languages series. http://cookingwithlanguages.com/free-sample/

Our books and tools have been designed to enhance young people's language-learning experience and can be used totally independently, (for pleasure), or as an educational compliment to any method they are currently using.

Unlike many traditional language learning books that dwell on detailed, grammatical explanations and structured learning, Cooking with Languages encourages instant comprehension of language structures and reinforces learning through practice and activities.

Cooking with Languages is not looking to fit into any existing market niche. It has created its own. The current market is bursting with children's language learning books and children's cookbooks. Cooking with Languages is introducing language learning whilst cooking.

Simple. Innovative. Fun. Effective.

Our mission is to encourage more children to embark on the wonderful path of language learning and help them to open new doors for their future.

Vivo en Mijas are a set of beautifully designed, hand drawn, bilingual books that provide children with a few simple phrases to learn before moving to Spain.

More details will be published on www.familylifeinspain.com very soon!

Testimonials

What people are saying about this book "Moving to Spain with Children"

"The Bible for any parent aiming to live in Spain. Up to date, clear and full of vitally important information, Lisa's book is a 'must-have' for any parent considering moving to Spain or here now with their children".

Nick Snelling, Gandia (Author)

"Essential reading for anyone considering moving to Spain with children, and in fact even without children, it is an excellent starting point. Balanced, factual and practical, the content gives the reader a real idea of where to start and what to expect. I wish it had been available when I moved here 6 years ago, and will undoubtedly save you time, money and stress. The personal stories highlight the pitfalls, and are all classic "welcome to Spain" tales, but give a truly balanced view assisting you in making a fully informed decision".

Kelly Lawlor, Vejer de la Frontera.

"For many years, Lisa Sadleir has been offering credible, independent counsel to families considering relocating to Spain. This book offers a valuable overview, including honest and clear advice on important issues for a successful relocation, including getting to grips with the Spanish language and making steps to integrate into the community beyond the expat bubble."

Andrew FORBES, Malaga.
(Journalist, Consultant & Editor)

"With so many factors to consider when moving to Spain, this book is indispensable reading for every family.

From critical factors such as healthcare, tax and gaining an NIE, to personal decisions such as schooling, languages and location, every major issue facing relocating families is well covered.

'Moving to Spain with Children' is an easy-to-read guide to make a thrilling challenge smoother and easier for anyone keen to reshape their lives."

Caroline Angus baker, New Zealand (Author).

"This is the missing manual we could have really done with 7 years ago, when researching our own family's relocation to Spain.

What starts as a simple dream ends up being incredibly complicated, expensive and full of unknowns.

Whilst there are many guidebooks available finding information specifically from a family perspective isn't easy.

It remains the best move we ever made, and if you are serious about making the move then you couldn't have a better guide in your hands than this book right here"

Maya Middlemiss, Denia, Alicante.

"Lisa has produced an easy to read, yet invaluable guide for 'Moving to Spain with Children'.

By asking the all important questions in a reflective way, (with lots of personal examples as well as stories and thoughts from other expats), Lisa has provided a valuable tool which can be read, shared with your children and discussed as a family.

The book is full of resources to increase your knowledge about moving to Spain, making the journey easier as you set off, on arrival and as the months in Spain spread into years. I am sure the book will be well thumbed!"

Ali Meehan, Malaga
(Founder of Costa Women www.costawomen.com)

"For many years, Lisa Sadleir has been offering credible, independent counsel to families considering relocating to Spain.

This book offers a valuable overview, including honest and clear advice on important issues for a successful relocation, including getting to grips with the Spanish language and making steps to integrate into the community beyond the expat bubble."

Andrew FORBES, Malaga
(Journalist, Consultant & Editor)

"Excellent common-sense guide to the dos and don'ts of moving to Spain with a family in tow.

Everything is covered from education to starting a business. My life would have been much easier if I had found a book like this 12 years ago instead of having to learn it all the hard way."

Fiona Pitt-Kethley, Cartagena, Murcia.

"This book is an honest account of what it's like to move to Spain with children: the good, the bad and the "mañana". It's packed with useful info and is a great tool for families to avoid the multiple pitfalls that can happen when thinking about living to Spain."

Maxine Raynor, Madrid
(Founder of www.moneysaverspain.com)

Index

CPSIA information can be obtained at www.ICGtesting.com
Printed in the USA
BVOW11s1100221015

423474BV00009B/188/P

9 781908 135605